6-99

BFI Modern Classics

D1330607

Edward Buscombe and Rob White
Series Editors

Advancing into its second century, the cinema is now a mature art form
with an established list of classics. But contemporary cinema is so
subject to every shift in fashion regarding aesthetics, morals and ideas
that judgments on the true worth of recent films are liable to be risky
and controversial; yet they are essential if we want to know where the
cinema is going and what it can achieve.

As part of the British Film Institute's commitment to the
promotion and evaluation of contemporary cinema, and in conjunction
with the influential BFI Film Classics series, BFI Modern Classics is a
series of books devoted to individual films of recent years. Distinguished
film critics, scholars and novelists explore the production and reception
of their chosen films in the context of an argument about the film's
quality and importance. Insightful, considered, often impassioned, these
elegant, well-illustrated books will set the agenda for debates about what
matters in modern cinema.

Don't Look Now

Mark Sanderson

BFI PUBLISHING

First published in 1996 by the
British Film Institute
21 Stephen St, London W1P 2LN

Copyright © Mark Sanderson 1996

The British Film Institute exists to promote
appreciation, enjoyment, protection and
development of moving image culture in and
throughout the whole of the United Kingdom.
Its activities include the National Film and
Television Archive; the National Film Theatre;
the Museum of the Moving Image;
the London Film Festival; the production and
distribution of film and video; funding and
support for regional activities; Library and
Information Services; Stills, Posters and
Designs; Research, Publishing and Education;
and the monthly *Sight and Sound* magazine.

Designed by Andrew Barron &
Collis Clements Associates

Typeset in Garamond Simoncini
by Fakenham Photosetting Ltd

Printed in Great Britain by Trinity Press,
Worcester

British Library Cataloguing-in-Publication Data
A catalogue record for this book is available
from the British Library
ISBN 0–85170–572–3

ST. HELENS
COLLEGE

791·43 72

85376

FEB 1997

LIBRARY

Contents

1 'I'm getting out of here.' *8*

2 'So many impressions to seize and hold.' *10*

3 'We've been trying to reach you.' *17*

4 'What is it you fear?' *24*

5 'The deeper we get the more Byzantine it gets.' *33*

6 'It's incredible you can't change your course.' *47*

7 'Nothing can take the place of the one that's gone.' *55*

8 'We're almost there.' *64*

9 'I know where we are now.' *71*

Credits *81*

Dedication

To Drew

Epigraph

Behind the corpse in the reservoir, behind the ghost on the links,
Behind the lady who dances and the man who madly drinks,
Under the look of fatigue, the attack of migraine and the sigh
There is always another story, there is more than meets the eye.

W. H. Auden. *Twelve Songs*, VIII

1 'I'm getting out of here.'

October 1995. A glossy commercial for the Ford Mondeo, featuring the actor David Threlfall as a man who leaves Venice because he misses his motor-car, is being shown on British television. *The Times* publishes its Top 100 Cult Films: the holder of position number five is a 'hypnotic chronicle of a death foretold' whose 'horrific, heart-stopping climax . . . gives you an even bigger shock second time around'. And *Haunted*, a ghost story starring Aidan Quinn and directed by Lewis Gilbert, is released in Britain. This pedestrian movie is enlivened by a seance attended by, among others, actress Hilary Mason. All three pay tribute to a film that was released in the same month twenty-two years ago: Nicolas Roeg's *Don't Look Now*.

The TV ad is a cunning pastiche of the movie: sun glinting on water, pigeons fluttering, thirty seductive seconds of perpetual motion. But, because cars would not sell if they were associated with corpses, the floating funeral cortège featured at the end of the film has been replaced by a wedding flotilla.

The four films that came higher in *The Times* list were, inevitably, Jim Sharman's *The Rocky Horror Picture Show* (1975); *Performance* (1970) – also directed by Roeg, with Donald Cammell; John Waters's *Pink Flamingos* (1972); and Todd Browning's *Freaks* (1932). The fact that Roeg's work figures twice in the top five testifies to his ability to hit a nerve – if not tap a vein – but the word 'cult' implies appreciation by a discriminating, or wilfully undiscriminating, few; and it is Roeg's uncompromising approach to his material that has occasionally caused him to be discriminated against. *Don't Look Now*, however, is one of his most accessible films and warrants a wider audience.

Hilary Mason plays Heather, the blind clairvoyant, in *Don't Look Now*. *Haunted* also refers to Roeg's film by way of plot, as well as echoing two other excellent British pictures of the 60s: Jack Clayton's *The Innocents* (1961) and Robert Wise's *The Haunting* (1963). It is not surprising that a film made in the mid-90s should hark back to one made in the 70s: once seen *Don't Look Now* is impossible to forget. If such disparate details are anything to go by, the film has made an indelible impression on the cinematic imagination and Roeg, certainly the greatest living director in Britain, deserves wider recognition.

There was still another month to go till my eleventh birthday when *Don't Look Now* was given its British release on 16 October 1973. I did not get to see it until it was first shown on television six years later (by the BBC on 30 December 1979) but even then, besides scaring the hell out of me, it suddenly made me appreciate the true potential of cinema. Having been made to study the multiple intricacies of irony at school, I soon saw that even the title of the film was ironic: what it was really saying was 'Look at Me!'

And *Don't Look Now* can be looked at in several ways: as a brilliant example of literary adaptation; as Gothic thriller; as black comedy; as an exploration of grief. As a teenager I was struck by the second; as a student I was impressed by the first; in my twenties I appreciated the third; and now, in my thirties, I have been made to realise by force of circumstances – the loss of someone close – just how sensitive and perceptive is its handling of bereavement. The flashy technique and dazzling style masks a strong undertow of genuine feeling that has often been overlooked. This is what makes *Don't Look Now* much more than a consummate chiller: there is genius in its treatment of genre.

Of course the movie is actually all of these things at the same time. Roeg is having his cake and eating it, sending up the conventions of ghost stories while investing them with new meaning; having it both ways is one of the hallmarks of a masterpiece. *Don't Look Now* is also a film about film. He uses light to illuminate life.

In the course of writing this book, I conducted interviews with Roeg and with Julie Christie. Extracts from these interviews form part of Chapter Three. An edited version of the complete interview with Roeg makes up Chapter Nine.

2 'So many impressions to seize and hold.'

Unlike the other chapter-titles in this book, the above line does not appear in the script of *Don't Look Now*. But it epitomises the film. It is taken from page 31 of the short story of the same name – its first three words providing the title – by Daphne du Maurier. The story was adapted for the screen by Allan Scott – who also collaborated with Roeg on *Castaway* (1986), *The Witches* (1989) and *Cold Heaven* (1990) – and Chris Bryant. First published in 1970, it tells the tale of John and Laura Baxter who, in an attempt to come to terms with the death of their daughter Christine, take a trip to Venice. Laura soon falls under the spell of two sisters, one of whom, a blind psychic called Heather, claims to have received a message from Christine telling her parents that they are in danger while they remain in the city. John pooh-poohs the suggestion and is subsequently murdered by a female dwarf. His final thought provides the last line: 'Oh God, what a bloody silly way to die . . . ' (p. 55). It is a superb conclusion: horror, embarrassment and comedy collide to produce a punch line with real punch. 'I wanted to clap when I read that line,' Roeg told *Sight and Sound* in 1973. 'I did think of keeping the line at one time, but at that point it would have been crazy for him to say anything.' Instead Roeg transforms the verbal flourish into an equivalent sequence of stunning visual bravura (analysed in Chapter Eight).

Even though the film is a remarkably faithful adaptation – in spirit as well as substance – some crucial changes have been made. When the story begins Christine has already died of meningitis. The opening sequence of the film – analysed shot by shot in Chapter Five – shows her drowning. Besides providing a much more dramatic start, this enables Roeg to set up the correspondence between the little girl and the dwarf straightaway, to emphasise the importance of water in the story and to ensure that the colour red is immediately associated with danger and death. In the story it is Laura who wears a 'scarlet coat' (p. 30) and Christine a 'blue dress' (p. 13). Roeg reverses the colours so that the dwarf can be a little red riding-hoodlum, and thus all the more conspicuous.

Christine is the Baxters' second child. Their first, Johnny, attends boarding school in England but is still the means by which his parents are separated. Du Maurier has the Baxters holidaying in Venice, which would be an odd choice if your daughter had drowned, so the film provides them with a pretext: John is overseeing the restoration of a church dedicated to Saint Nicholas. In case we miss the point Bishop Barbarrigo (Massimo Serato) – who does not appear in the story – tells Laura that Saint Nicholas is the patron saint of scholars and children: 'An interesting combination, don't you think?'. He is, of course, also known as Santa Claus, whose garb is traditionally red. John will soon be seeking help at the police station, 'the nick', and will eventually be killed

by the devilish dwarf, the ultimate personification of evil being Old Nick. And Nicolas is Roeg's Christian name. The film creates such an atmosphere of the paranormal and the paranoid that there seems no room for harmless coincidence.

'Christine is the Baxters' second child.'

After Laura tells John about the weird sister's message they are woken in the middle of the night by a telephone call from England. Communication – getting in touch, bridging the gap, crossing the threshold – is one of the main themes of *Don't Look Now*. In the story Johnny has suspected appendicitis but in the film he has been injured during a fire practice. Such drills are supposed to prevent accidents not cause them: one example of how a well-intentioned attempt to achieve something ends up precipitating the direct opposite. A source of tragedy certainly, but also the mainspring of black comedy.

Laura immediately assumes that Heather's portentous message refers to this accident; she has lost one child and does not want to lose another. She is wrong. Roeg, like du Maurier, is in two minds about the Scottish sisters, seeing them as both silly and sinister. On the first page

Laura meets two sisters who claim to be able to contact her dead child. 'Helping people in Roeg's films is always dangerous.'

of the story Laura tells John, 'They're not old girls at all . . . They're male twins in drag.' They are portrayed with great skill on the screen by Mason (Heather) who is English and Clelia Matania (Wendy) who is Italian. The suspicion that they may be tweedy lesbians is given a comic twist by Roeg when he has them inadvertently entering the male lavatories in the restaurant. Wendy, the sighted sister, has something in her eye and so neither of them can see where they are going. Laura's decision to help them prompts Heather's confession that she has 'seen' Christine.

Helping people in Roeg's films is always dangerous. Turner (Mick Jagger) helps Chas (James Fox) in *Performance* by granting him sanctuary but ends up being shot. The Aborigine (David Gumpilil) in *Walkabout* (1970) saves the lives of the girl (Jenny Agutter) and boy (Roeg's son Lucien John) but ends up hanging from a tree. And John's attempts to help what he thinks is a distressed little girl only succeed in getting him hacked to death. All three selfless acts turn out to be different forms of suicide – half-wished, half-feared – which, depending on your point of view, can either be seen as the utter loss of self or the ultimate act of self-possession. It would seem that the only way to survive is to keep yourself to yourself – but that way, as Jack McCann (Gene Hackman) finds to his cost in *Eureka* (1982), madness lies. You have to keep trying to reach out. As E. M. Forster wrote in *Howard's End*: 'Only connect!'

But are the sisters helpful or harmful? Du Maurier's sceptical 'a seance in the living room, tambourines appearing out of thin air' (p. 52) finds it equivalent (when Laura asks, 'Can you ever contact people?') in Heather's outburst, 'They all want a lot of mumbo-jumbo about ectoplasm and holding hands', which is soon unconsciously echoed by John: 'I'm not going to get involved with two neurotic old women in a session of mumbo-jumbo. No way.' Holding hands is an important gesture throughout the film.

It is essential to mark out one's territory – the familiar haunt of such ghost writers as M. R. James, Henry James and James Herbert – so that one can begin to undermine it. John's 'sudden rather unkind picture of the two sisters putting on headphones in their bedroom, listening for a coded message from poor Christine' (p. 51) transfers to the screen as the sudden cut to the scene in which the two sisters are laughing their heads off in a hotel room. It suggests that, along with the Church of St Nicholas, they may be phonies: 'I'm restoring a fake,' says John. But the viewer has no idea what has caused their laughter: it may be a memory evoked by one of the photographs of the children; it may be something one of them has said. Their cackling could be the horrid laughter of Jacobean tragedy or the helpless giggling of two sweet old ladies. Either way, whether they are guilty or innocent, the startling scene is simultaneously scary and amusing. Both du Maurier and Roeg want to keep us guessing, to unsettle us, thus enhancing the creepy atmosphere. In the story the hotel manager is always helpful and the policeman always reassuring but in the film they soon cease to be so. As John becomes ever more distraught the people he turns to for help – those ordinarily expected to be of service – only increase his sense of discomfort.

Alfred Hitchcock, like du Maurier, was a master of unease and filmed three of her works: *Jamaica Inn* (1939), *Rebecca* (1940) and *The Birds* (1963). In each case it is not just a question of plot: her insistence on sound and vision makes her an intensely cinematic writer. In 'Don't Look Now' her repeated use of the word 'glittering' to describe Venice – 'a bright façade put on for show, glittering by sunlight' (p. 25) – is matched by Roeg's repeated use of shots of sunshine reflected in water, windows and mirrors. The effect is literally dazzling, often making the viewer squint or think about holding up a hand to shield the eyes: don't look now. And her attention to the noise things make – 'there was a crunch of feet on the gravel' (p. 11); 'he heard the quick patter of feet' (p. 20); 'their heels made a ringing sound on the pavement and the rain splashed from the gutterings above' (p. 20) – is literally echoed by Roeg on an exceptionally complex soundtrack. It is a truism that the unsighted can hear better than the sighted: Heather – who, like Tiresias, can also 'see' better – tells John that she likes Venice for this very reason: 'It's so safe for me to walk . . . the sound changes you see as you come to a canal and the echoes off the walls are so clear.' *Don't Look Now* reveals Roeg's admiration for Hitchcock, and, indeed, contains one direct tribute to him. The jump-cut at the end of the opening sequence in which Laura's short, sharp scream merges with the drill as it pierces the stone of St Nicholas's mirrors the cut in *The Thirty-Nine Steps* (1935) when a woman's terrified scream merges with that of a steam train's whistle.

It is Hollywood tradition for the original writer to scream 'foul' when they finally see what has been done to their brainchild. After du Maurier had seen '*Don't Look Now*' she wrote to Roeg congratulating him on having captured the emotions of John and Laura. A perfect riposte to those critics who accuse Roeg of coldness. If his masterpiece does chill the blood, it also warms the heart in its anatomy of love and loss.

———

Some time after their daughter, Christine, has drowned while playing in the garden, John and Laura Baxter are in Venice where John is in charge of restoring the Church of St Nicholas. One lunchtime in a restaurant with John, Laura goes to the aid of two ageing Scottish sisters, Heather and Wendy. The former, who is blind, tells Laura that she can 'see' Christine and that her daughter is happy. Laura, somewhat shaken, returns to her table, faints and is taken to hospital.

She recounts Heather's message to John and, although this offends his stubborn rationalism, he allows himself to be convinced that his wife has made a complete recovery. On the way back to their hotel Laura insists on visiting a church to pray and is not deterred when their launch is forced to make a detour because of a murder. That evening, after passionately making love, the couple go out for dinner but get lost in a maze of alleyways. Momentarily separated from Laura, John sees what he thinks is a small child dressed in a similar red mackintosh to the one Christine was wearing when she died. The next day, much to John's displeasure, Laura attends a seance with the sisters. John, in his cups, tries to interrupt the seance but, mistaken for a Peeping Tom, is forced to flee. Laura returns with a warning that John is in danger while he remains in Venice and he half-heartedly agrees to take some time off work. That night they are woken by a telephone call from their son's

school in England: Johnny has been hurt in an accident. The next
morning Laura flies to England but, after nearly falling to his death in
St Nicholas's, John sees her sailing past with the two sisters. Unable to
find the sisters' *pensione*, and afraid that Laura has been abducted, he
goes to the police who are busy investigating a series of murders. When
he leaves the police station he is followed by a detective and unwittingly
manages to lead him to the sisters' hotel: the women have checked out
because of reports of a Peeping Tom. A call to England makes John
realise his mistake – his wife and son are fine – and he promises to have
dinner with Laura when she returns to Venice that evening. However,
by this time, the police have already arrested the sisters. Confused and
contrite, John escorts Heather back to her new hotel. Soon after their
arrival she goes into another trance and sends Wendy after him with a

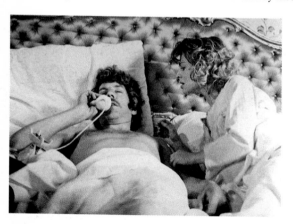

A telephone call
from England
brings news that
the Baxters' other
child, Johnny, has
been hurt.

further warning: 'Let him not go!' Outside the hotel she meets Laura
who races after her husband but cannot save him. John, having seen the
girl in red once more, and assuming that she is fleeing an attacker,
chases after her and corners her in a ruined palazzo. She turns out to
be an aged female dwarf and proceeds to hack him to death. Laura and
Johnny, accompanied by the sisters, glide down the Grand Canal in a
funeral barge.

3 'We've been trying to reach you.'

Although two other artists – real-life couple Natalie Wood and Robert Wagner – were mentioned for the parts of John and Laura Baxter, Roeg had Julie Christie and Donald Sutherland in mind from the very beginning. 'I just thought Julie was ideal,' Roeg told me in January 1996, 'Her person, her manner, her acting all made her perfect but she was working for the McGovern presidential campaign in America. I liked the idea of an English woman and an American man, rather than two English or two American people, the idea of fitting but misfitting, coming from two totally different backgrounds but living on common ground – but Donald was not available either. He was shooting a movie. Then, damn me, within a couple of weeks McGovern was defeated by

Nixon and Donald's film collapsed. It just seemed meant to be. I was held up for a bit but somehow I felt that they would come to the movie anyway.'

Nicolas Roeg thought Christie ideal for the role of Laura.

But no matter how much he wanted Sutherland he was not prepared to negotiate. Michael Feeney Callan in his biography of Julie Christie quotes Sutherland:

I phoned Nic Roeg from Florida after I had read the script of *Don't Look Now* and said that I wanted to sit down and talk to him about it. He said: 'What do you want to talk about?' I replied with this long speech about how I felt that ESP was a positive part of our lives and therefore we should make *Don't Look Now* a more educative sort of film, that the characters should in some way benefit from ESP and not just be destroyed by it. Nic said: 'That's not how I feel.' I said, 'Well, what do you feel?' and he just said: 'What's in the script, do you want to do it or not?' I asked if we could talk about it and he said 'No.' So I said, 'Well, if you want to put it that way, yes I do . . .' and I just went and obeyed orders and had a wonderful time. (p. 132)

'We did speak on the telephone,' said Roeg, 'Donald had many, many thoughts about the script and I said something like, "I want you to be John but I can't agree with what you're saying." There was no great disagreement. I think we were just testing each other. In the end he arrived and was terrific. I remember him saying that he would like to have a different image and to change his hair. Normally I'm chary of wigs but Donald had this extraordinary wigmaker in Hollywood whom he'd been to before – he's retired now, I think it was one of his last jobs – and he made him this fantastic wig which totally altered Donald's appearance and stayed on under the water with no trouble at all. You still can't tell it's a wig. It was an excellent idea because I didn't want them to be Donald and Julie but John and Laura.'

'I haven't a clue why Nic wanted me,' Christie explained to me (12 January 1996). 'All I knew was that I wanted to work with him. I was impressed by the script – it was unusual in the way it came at things tangentially.' It was not the first time they had worked together: Roeg had shot Christie in such films as François Truffaut's *Fahrenheit*

451 (1966) and John Schlesinger's *Far from the Madding Crowd* (1967); indeed the photography is the most interesting thing about them. 'Nic has an unusual eye and an unusual mind,' continued Christie: 'As a director he is quite secretive, not enormously collaborative, but this is the way he succeeds. The whole film could have gone completely haywire, it was a bit of a risk, but I don't like run-of-the-mill stuff. In the event the risk paid off. Whatever else may be said about it, it is certainly technically interesting.'

Filming began in England in December 1972. A week later it broke off for Christmas then resumed in January 1973 for seven more weeks in Italy. The Baxters' peculiar Hertfordshire home belonged in real life to David Tree who plays headmaster Anthony Babbage in the film. 'He was a charming man,' according to Roeg. 'He'd started his acting career just before the Second World War but had been wounded. He was a descendant of the actor-manager Sir Herbert Beerbohm Tree.' The Venice locations included the Europa Hotel, but the Baxters' suite really belonged to the Bauer Grunwald whose larger rooms allowed the camera to be pulled back. 'I actually stayed in a villa belonging to friends in Giudecca,' Christie told me: 'It had an amazing formal garden – even the vegetables were laid out formally. You would open these magnificent Venetian wrought-iron gates at the bottom of it and there, suddenly, would be not earth but water. It was quite surreal . . . I remember walking through Venice at night with Nic and Tony, the photographer. We were half-cut and wandered through all these mysterious, damp alleyways looking at the reflection of the water on the wet stone and the reflection of the buildings in the canals. I loved it but I've never been back.'

———

'Superior physchological [*sic*] thriller. Bright prospects', said *Variety*. Perhaps the sub-editor had also seen the movie and was suffering from shock. 'No matter what happens to this crackerjack chiller commercially

– and the potential outlook is decidedly good – it should firmly establish director Nicholas [oops again] Roeg as the latest cult hero.' *Don't Look Now* came out in the same year as *The Exorcist* – which perhaps partly explains the rosy economic forecast – but the reviewer chose to compare it favourably with *Rosemary's Baby* (1968) instead, praising the script, performances, camerawork and editing. The final paragraph reads: 'Superlatives, by the way, should not distract or make one expect too much too soon. Pic's ultimate, lasting impact comes long after it's ended and the thoughts it has triggered have had time to develop and seize the imagination.'

The *New Yorker* judged the film to be 'the fanciest, most carefully assembled enigma yet seen on the screen'. Vincent Canby in *The New York Times* was sniffier: 'A fragile soap bubble of a film. It has a shiny

Roeg directing Sutherland and Christie in a love scene which was to cause widespread controversy.

surface that reflects all sorts of colors and moods, but after watching it for a while, you realize you're looking not into it, but through it and out the other side. The bubble doesn't burst, it slowly collapses, and you may feel, as I did, that you've been had.'

But Canby was not entirely negative. Roeg 'gets a great performance from Venice, which is all wintery grays, blues and blacks, the color of the pigeons that are always underfoot.' The 'beautifully photographed love scene' received a special mention too but then Canby goes and spoils it all by assuming that the cross-cutting between the love-making and dressing for dinner is 'essentially comic': 'The point, I guess, is that if you can see into the future, it's often difficult to keep your mind on the present, no matter what you're doing.' Canby, evidently, did not look at how the scene relates to the rest of the film. Perhaps he had soap in his eye.

The love scene caused problems before *Don't Look Now* was released on both sides of the Atlantic. 'People didn't do scenes like that in those days', Christie commented. 'There were no available examples, no role models, and I did find it very difficult. I just went blank and Nic shouted instructions. I hardly knew Donald then either but apart from being a bloody good actor he's a responsible one and took responsibility for the scene, helping me through it.' If any further proof were needed of the powerful physical chemistry between Christie and Sutherland, it came twenty years later when they were reunited for *The Railway Station Man*, an adaptation of the novel by Jennifer Johnston, shown by the BBC on 30 December 1993. 'All the performances are impressive, but Christie is superb,' said the *Sunday Times* (then it would – I was the previewer).

'We cannot see humping. We cannot see the rise and fall between thighs,' the American censor advised Roeg. 'I honestly couldn't remember if there was any rise and fall,' Roeg told *Time Out* in 1976.

I went away and examined the sequence very carefully, took out just nine frames and sent it back. They scrutinised it and found

absolutely nothing they could object to. If someone goes up, you cut and the next time you see them and they're in a different position, you obviously fill in the gaps for yourself. But, technically speaking, there was no 'humping' in that scene.

Even so the film was given an R – i.e. restricted – rating. The kiss of death at the box-office.

In England *Don't Look Now* was given an X – i.e. adults only – certificate. On 5 October 1973 the *Daily Mail*, true to form, burbled: 'one of the frankest love scenes ever to be filmed is likely to plunge lovely Julie Christie into the biggest censorship row since *Last Tango in Paris*.' It did not happen. The non-story annoyed Roeg, as did rumours that a collection of out-takes from the scene was doing the rounds of Wardour Street. After more than two decades, when far more explicit footage has been seen on television, both items now seem like the work of an astute publicist.

British critics, especially the serious ones, liked what they saw. Because *Don't Look Now* was Roeg's third film to be released, they inevitably judged it in relation to *Performance* and *Walkabout*. 'The three films form an astonishing trilogy querying the whole conception of "civilisation",' wrote Tom Milne in the *Monthly Film Bulletin*. 'They also put Nicolas Roeg right up at the top as a film-maker.' Penelope Houston, in *Sight and Sound*, saw the film as 'the inevitable culmination of what . . . looks to be Roeg's special theme: a man in some way willing his own death'. She concluded: 'Roeg deploys subtle powers of direction and Hitchcockian misdirection, along with some plain hocus-pocus . . . It is not all, however, done with the camera. All the leading performances are striking.' Gordon Gow, in *Films and Filming*, enjoyed the 'clever variations upon traditional suspense ploys' and the use of slow motion ('matched only by Peckinpah') but in the end decided that 'although the film hardly aspires to the comment upon human behaviour that was so essential to Roeg's work in *Performance* and *Walkabout*, it is nevertheless a thriller of some depth'.

If pretension lies in the gap between one's goal and one's grasp,

Don't Look Now is not pretentious in the least. Roeg achieves exactly what he set out to do – to explore the minds of a grief-stricken couple using the conventions of a Gothic novel. Both brain and book must deal with horror; in both cases it is a question of learning the tropes. Today's audience has the luxury of viewing the film in the context of Roeg's later work. The fact that none of it has reached the same level of achievement even though rehearsing the same themes – for example Newton's separation from his family in *The Man Who Fell to Earth* (1976) – only underlines to what degree *Don't Look Now* succeeds. It is the quintessence of Roeg, his personal eureka, and like Jack McCann, misunderstood and mistreated, he seems destined to struggle on and on in search of that elusive something else.

4 'What is it you fear?'

The first Gothic novel is generally taken to be Horace Walpole's *The Castle of Otranto* (1765). Indeed it is subtitled 'A Gothic Story'. Walpole originally used the word to suggest 'medieval' but the meaning of 'Gothic' soon slid into a catch-all term for the bizarre goings-on in the novel: ghosts, sinister statues, strange visions and uncontrollable passions – love, agony and despair – suffered against a backdrop of graveyards, subterranean chambers and ruins. The secret stuff of nightmares was splattered across the page with panache. Fictional fear became highly fashionable.

Like *The Castle of Otranto*, *Don't Look Now* is set in Italy and features a climactic stabbing. Venice – its Renaissance masterpieces and Gothic façades sinking slowly into the sea – is the perfect setting for a story of physical and psychic ruin and restoration. A sign on the wall of St Nicholas's reads 'Venice in Peril' and John Baxter works to save it. But the title of the film could just as well be 'Peril in Venice' and John, in spite of being warned, is unable to save himself.

The Church of St Nicholas is a continual source of trouble to John – professionally and personally. The scene in which he wrestles with a hideous stone statue outside – both of them in constant danger of falling to the ground – prefigures his eventual death at the hands of the dwarf and the intervening near-death experience inside the church when the cradle carrying him as he examines the mosaic collapses. Gargoyles were intended to ward off evil not attract it.

Venice is a city of bridges: constant reminders that the sea is inexorably reclaiming the land that was once reclaimed from it. Water, water is everywhere. It is a giver of life and a giver of death. John, like Christine, will soon be out of his depth, crossing over from this world to the next. A floating zone of fleeting impressions, it is the natural place to find the supernatural. Wendy's mermaid brooch – a mythical creature who could live on land and in water – is a recurrent motif, its shape even discernible in the map of Venice behind Inspector Longhi's desk.

The point is that Italy is not the Baxters' normal environment. They are strangers in a strange land, without the familiar fabric of places and possessions that lends security to our everyday lives. John can more or less get by in Italian but Laura cannot: the language is never subtitled which adds to our sense of isolation. And the misunderstanding works both ways: when John is trying to trace the sisters, the two women who run the hotel – wearing sinister dark glasses even though indoors – do not know what he is talking about; and when Laura is picked up at the airport the policeman's sign reads 'Signora Baster' which would sound to Italian ears like Signora Basta, Mrs Enough. And there are enough misses in store for everyone.

The Baxters have run away from home, from the scene of personal tragedy, but even in Venice they keep on running. They run out of the Gothic cathedral where Laura lights six candles for Christine (one of which, ominously, is snuffed out by a draught). Late as a consequence, they run to their appointment with Bishop Barbarrigo. In fact John starts running in the first moments of the film when he senses something is wrong. In the last moments of his life John runs after the fleeing manikin and Laura runs after them both. In running away from their pain, they are actually racing to meet it.

John is also running away from himself, refusing to acknowledge that he may have second sight. Using only half his mind – it is no coincidence that the face in the mosaic is only half complete – being wilfully blind, it is no wonder that he keeps losing his bearings. And Venice, with its labyrinth of alleys, courtyards, bridges and dead-ends, is very easy to get lost in. En route to the restaurant for dinner the Baxters lose their way in the dark. A passageway ends abruptly at the water's edge. A couple of white rats scuttle to and fro, searching for food in a giant laboratory maze. 'I know this place,' murmurs John. A sudden cry – halfway between a scream and a death rattle – breaks the eerie silence. A man closes a shutter creating a virtual blackout. John becomes separated from Laura: it is a moment of palpable panic. He then experiences an immediate flashback of the last few seconds, but this

'In running away from their pain, they are actually racing to meet it.'

time round he also catches a glimpse of something red. It is over almost before it has begun; John is reunited with Laura. As if by magic they know where they are and find themselves back in 'the real world'. It is a sequence worthy of Hitchcock, one in which external events suddenly reveal the workings of the protagonist's mind. John gets lost searching for Laura in the sisters' hotel. The police station is one vast corridor with dozens of doors: John does not know which knob to turn. The network of sulci – the serpentine grooves on the surface of the brain – resembles a labyrinth: in one sense the whole film takes place inside John's head.

Death in Venice (1971) takes place in summer, *Don't Look Now* in winter. It makes sense for a chiller to be chilly: people shiver from the cold as well as fear. It seeps into the bones, restricts movement, freeze-frames living flesh. The gargoyle is stone-cold; John, finally face to face with the dwarf, cannot move. He is petrified, a human statue. Venice, out of season, is as cold as the grave. The characters are forever dealing with hats, coats and scarves – struggling to keep the cold out of their clothes as well as their hearts – their speech producing plumes of condensation in the frigid air. The sight of Laura's breath wreathing about her as she stands to attention on the funeral barge at the very end of the film underlines her vulnerability but at the same time it also hints at the new-found vitality beneath her widow's weeds and is strangely touching. She – and Julie Christie – has never looked so beautiful: mourning indeed becomes her.

If coldness is macabre it can be melancholy too. There is something intrinsically depressing about a deserted tourist trap (from a film-maker's point of view, though, the absence of rubbernecks makes life much easier). The fairground opposite John and Laura's hotel is shut up. Inside the lobby the furniture is shrouded in dust-sheets. Everywhere is closing down, there is a pervasive sense of an ending. The crumbling stone of the *palazzi* and the dirty water of the gondola-free canals paint a dismal backdrop. Economically and emotionally, winter is a season of discontent. Even the good Lord seems to have checked out: 'Do churches belong to God?' asks the bishop, staring at a headless statue.

'But he doesn't seem to care about them . . . Does he have other priorities?' The desolation of the city mirrors that of Laura who hopes that the sisters will cure her emptiness and pain. Heather tells John that Wendy hates Venice: 'She says it's like a city in aspic left over from a dinner party and all the guests are dead and gone. It frightens her, too many shadows.'

The whole tenor of *Don't Look Now* echoes that of John Donne's 'A Nocturnall upon S. Lucies Day, being the shortest day': 'The Sunne is spent, and now his flasks / Send forth light squibs, no constant rayes; / The worlds whole sap is sunke.' Donne, like Laura, feels as if he has been reduced to 'A quintessence even from nothingnesse, / From dull privations and leane emptinesse'. And when, in his abortive attempt to rescue Christine, John plunges into the icy pond, he too finds himself 're-begot / Of absence, darkness, death; things which are not'. (There is no more final end-rhyme in metaphysical poetry.)

The finality of death is what makes it so fearful. Gothic aims to provoke this fear, to play with it and wallow in it. Strategies for dealing with it are outside its terror-tory. Its shock-in-trade is frisson not reason. *Don't Look Now* examines ways of coming to terms with death only to show that most of them – work, drink, denial, running and religion – are useless. Hence the black comedy.

Genuine Gothic is just black. It chooses to ignore the laughter in slaughter, but what passes for Gothic today has degenerated into camp, a steady stream of killing jokes that sneers at the conventions of the genre while celebrating their perennial power. There is only one moment of camp in *Don't Look Now*, when Heather – the medium with the message – brushes her fingers along a grille in the cathedral, smiling to herself and going 'Ah! Ah! Ah!' John, stupidly, is afraid of being seen by the blind woman and hides his face. He won't look now which is why he jumps when Laura touches him. Seeing his hands over his face she assumes he is pretending to pray: 'Hypocrite!' Is he a whited sepulchre or simply embarrassed by such a public display of religious ecstasy? Whatever, the image is significant because once again the psychic is viewed behind bars. The next day Laura speaks to Heather through the bars of a gate at St Nicholas's. The strong verticals prefigure her eventual arrest following John's accusations.

The Gothic is at its thickest during the seance, which is genuinely terrifying. Any potential for nervous giggling – 'Are your legs crossed?' (marked by the briefest of trills in the score) – is ruthlessly suppressed. The comedy is kept outside the room where John is blundering about in the dark. Heather's orgasmic cries create a situation in which the other guests mistake him for a Peeping Tom. But he does not see anything. John's Italian mysteriously deserts him – the communicating is happening on the other side of the door – and he is forced to flee again. As Heather kneads her chest – the camera moving quickly across the bed to her feet and then rising above her as though an approaching spirit – a crying baby can be heard. Is the child in another room? Is it hungry? Has it been summoned from the picture of the Madonna and Child on the wall? Or is it the voice of a ghost, an unquiet soul forever parted from the maternal breast? The uncertainty only increases our insecurity. In the same way, the fact that Heather is not given time to reveal what she has 'seen' further tightens the screws. Laura still has not been reunited with her daughter.

Whether Heather is genuine or not, Christine's message turns out to be horribly real. The dead can see what we cannot – and that includes ourselves. The sensation of being watched – out of curiosity, perversity or hostility – is unpleasant, enough to make the hairs on the back of one's neck stand up. In Gothic the eyes of a portrait (actually belonging, say, to the misbegotten manservant standing behind it) follow you about the room; the ahead of a statue turns after you. In *Don't Look Now* the Venetians always have their eyes on John and Laura, watching them from the security of their own homes, from the windows of cafés and from their place of work. And they never, ever, say anything: the lavatory attendant in the restaurant, the person throwing dirty water into the canal, the man closing the shutters, all remain silent. It is as if they know something we do not and are keeping out of trouble, experts at turning the cold shoulder. When the sisters first encounter Laura, Wendy apologises to her for gawping: 'Country people always stare.' For all we know Heather may possess the evil eye rather than second sight.

In du Maurier's short story John says 'don't look now' because the sisters are watching the Baxters. The three words are a double-edged warning: avert your eyes because you may be caught staring or you might see something you would rather not. *Don't Look Now* is a head-turning movie. It is worth any number of second looks and features characters who are forever looking back over their shoulders. Its paranoia is so infectious that a flurry of pigeons is enough to create panic. John, especially, feels as though something or someone is creeping up on him. It turns out to be Time's wingèd chariot but before then his fears for his wife bring about a physical embodiment of his mental condition: when he leaves the police station he is followed by Detective Sabbione.

The fact that John seeks the help of the Italian police voluntarily but leaves their headquarters under suspicion is a further Hitchcockian irony and Roeg exploits all its potential for black comedy. However, Inspector Longhi (who shares his name with the white lily often seen at funerals) does take John's concern for Laura seriously, even though he is leading the hunt for a serial killer.

The paths of the Baxters, the Inspector and the murderer first cross when John and Laura are returning from the hospital but Laura has already left Venice by the time we see a corpse being winched out of the water – to the same cello music that accompanies Christine's drowning. Although John and Laura hear a murder taking place when they get lost in the dark, the only killing we actually witness in the film is the murder of John.

A marauding murderer is a splendid Gothic character. The idea that one is at large is enough to make anyone think that they keep catching something out of the corner of their eye. The malicious munchkin not only represents John's premonitions of unspecified danger but also ensures that they are realised in a gruesomely specific manner. Instead of warning him off, the flashing red draws him on to his doom.

Memories of his daughter blind him to the meaning of her message. In his grief he hopes and hopes that somehow the fleeing figure is his daughter; in any event, he wants to help the damsel in distress – he is her 'friend'. But she is a fiend and wields her knife. Venice proves to be the last resort.

John's bloody end is pure Gothic horror. It is painful, protracted, terrifying and humiliating. And it certainly got to Sutherland: 'We shot the climax last and I knew I was going to die in it and I became literally convinced that I would die, and dying began to feel almost like a sexual rite' (Callan, p. 133). Red holds a fatal fascination for Roeg. When Joey (Anthony Valentine), hiding beneath the covers – don't look now! – is shot by Chas in *Performance*, the whole screen turns red. When the boy in *Walkabout* finally succumbs to sunstroke the whole screen turns red

A corpse is winched out of the water. A murderer is on the loose in Venice.

again, the red you see when you look at the sun through your closed eyelids. Both Gothic and cinema offer magical mystery tours. If Stanley Kubrick explored the metaphysical conundrum that 'murder' is 'red rum' (red room) in reverse in *The Shining* (1980) – and 'red' rhymes with 'dead' – *Don't Look Now* reveals that the letters of 'Roeg', looked at another way, spell out 'gore'.

––––––––––

Theatre folk are famously superstitious, which is why – ever since 7 August 1606 when the boy-actor playing Lady Macbeth at the Globe Theatre dropped dead of fever in mid-performance – they have referred to *Macbeth* as 'that play', 'the unmentionable' or 'the Scottish play'. According to *Brewer's Theatre*, if an actor says the original title of the play in the dressing room: 'he or she must immediately leave the room, turn around three times, break wind or spit, knock on the door, and ask permission to re-enter. Alternatively, the line "Angels and ministers of grace defend us", from *Hamlet* (I, iv), may be quoted'. No one is sure what attracted the persistent bad luck in the first place but the witches' curses provide a likely explanation. As for *Don't Look Now,* this particular tale of weird Scottish sisters has attracted its own cluster of spooky correspondences. Natalie Wood, although she never got to play Laura, drowned during the shooting of *Brainstorm* (1983) in 1981. In 1979 Julie Christie found her friend's son drowned in a pond on her farm in Cefn-Y-Coed, Wales. He was twenty-two months old. And Nicholas Salter, who played the accident-prone Johnny, was later to die as a young adult in the notorious wing of Brixton prison known to inmates as 'Fraggle Rock'.

5 'The deeper we get the more Byzantine it gets.'

The opening sequence of *Don't Look Now*, which includes the titles, contains more than one hundred shots but lasts just seven minutes. It is a textbook example of compression and encapsulation, giving the unwitting viewer virtually the whole ensuing film in a nutshell. It also serves as a warning: blink and you'll miss it. In other words keep your eyes peeled. Do look now.

The only way to appreciate the complexity of the sequence and the dexterity with which it is compiled is to analyse it shot by shot, to hold up to the light each tile of the filmic mosaic.

1. Rain falling on the surface of a pond. The sound of distant thunder. Water is the dominant element of the movie; falling a recurrent motif. Precipitation can mean a headlong fall as well as rain. The weather is bad and something bad is about to happen. It is going to be a truly miserable day. The camera zooms in to a close-up of the raindrops as they shatter the surface tension of the pond. Water trickles on the soundtrack. The title – in aquamarine lettering – is superimposed on the image. The inverted commas round it are significant, acknowledging the film's literary source but also suggesting that the whole movie is a quotation. They are an ironic distancing device and signal self-reflexivity. We are about to watch a picture about watching, a film about film.
2. Dissolve – what could be more natural in a waterwork? – to a shimmering pattern of light and dark, the very essence of cinema. Church bells softly ring the knell of parting day. At this stage it is impossible to work out what exactly is being shown. In fact it will be some twenty-five minutes before we realise that it is the shuttered window of the Baxters' hotel room in Venice. The camera can penetrate these defences against prying eyes and tracks up from the dazzling water to the sun that is reflecting on it. Someone – it turns out to be John Baxter – is humming. Already a fluid approach to time and location has been adopted; a predilection for looking through windows revealed.

A story about being put in the frame – the sisters are suspected of kidnapping Laura, John is put under surveillance by the police – is being told by framing.

3. Blackout. Silence. What has happened to the man who was humming? Is he asleep or dead? Was the previous shot a premonition, a flash-forward, a memory or a dream? The break marks a shift in time and location.

4. Long shot. A little golden-haired girl in a shiny red mac is playing with a wheelbarrow. She has her back to the camera and is walking away from it. A white horse canters into and out of shot, whinnying. It is a scene of pastoral innocence. An elegiac tune is picked out on a piano, hesitantly, as if a child were practising.

5. A golden-haired boy dressed in blue jeans and a blue baseball jacket rides his bike through the grass in the low, pale, winter sunshine.

6. Long shot. The little girl is playing with a doll. She disappears behind a tree.

7. Cut. Low-angle shot. The doll is not a Sindy or Barbie, as might be expected, but a male. It speaks: 'Action Man patrol. Open fire.'

8. Close-up of the doll. The girl pulls its string: 'This is your commandant speaking.' She picks up a red and white ball and throws it.

9. The ball lands in some water. Splash.

10. The girl walks along the edge of a pond, the camera tracking her from left to right. 'Mortar attack begin.' She sets foot on a narrow wooden bridge. A doll's house can be seen in the foreground. It has blue walls and a red roof. The doll's tin hat falls into the water. Plop.

11. The girl looks back – an action that is repeated by virtually every character time and again. (Even Charlie Chaplin in the poster on the wall next to St Nicholas's is looking over his right shoulder.) She goes back to where the hat fell in.

12. Long shot. Little boy blue cycles directly towards the camera with a branch in his right hand. A tree trunk fills the right-hand side of the screen. Is someone hiding behind it, spying on the child? The boy disappears behind the tree, repeatedly coming into and going out of shot

as he passes other trees. Now you see him, now you don't.

13. Low-angle shot. The girl is standing on the bridge with her back to the camera. The doll's house is in the foreground, a real house in the background. It, too, seems to be of two different colours: half white and half brown. Rooks, traditional presagers of doom, caw on the soundtrack.

14. The girl is crouching down. She leans out over the pond. The camera drops to her reflection in the water. The piano music stops.

15. Close-up of the flames in the fireplace of the Baxters' drawing room. The camera pulls back to reveal the back of a woman dressed in blue who is sitting reading and the right profile of Donald Sutherland who is sitting at a desk looking at slides of a church. A red-hooded figure is sitting in one of its pews. The only sound is the whirr-click of the projector.

In the opening sequence of the film, John and Laura are oblivious to the tragedy unfolding outside.

16. Close-up of Sutherland.

17. A complex shot. One third of it (on the left) is of the woman's back, the remaining two-thirds is taken up by the projector screen on which can be seen in close-up a slide of the church, tilted at an oblique angle. The positions of the woman in blue and the figure in red are identical. The slide changes: the next one is at an even crazier angle. The third is on the level, taken crouching down in the nave.

18. Close-up of the slide. Little red riding-hood is plainly visible in the pew on the right. This image of a magnificent stained-glass window is about to be stained.

19. Close-up of Sutherland. His eyes move right towards the woman.

20. She is reading on the floor by the fire with her back to us.

21. Close-up of Sutherland: 'What are you reading?'

'Nothing is what it seems': different kinds of seeing are explored throughout the film.

22. She turns. Julie Christie sighs and closes her books: 'I was just trying to find the answer to a question Christine was asking me.' She drops the book on the sofa and picks up another. 'If the world's round . . .'

23. Medium shot of Sutherland. Christie: '. . . why is a frozen pond flat?'

24. Close-up of the same slide. The camera moves to the right and rests on the red-hooded figure.

25. Sutherland smiles. He leans over and takes the slide out of the projector: 'Hmmm. It's a good question.' He examines the transparency and switches on the light-box.

26. Close-up of the slide on the box. Sutherland straightens it up, trying to work out what the red thing is. The camera zooms in on it. A trill of four flute notes breaks the silence.

27. Christine, reflected in the water, runs along the edge of the pond from left to right.

28. The boy emerges from behind a Douglas fir and cycles towards the camera. It focuses on the front wheel.

29. Christine steps in a puddle.

30. A dazzling close-up. The front wheel of the bike smashes a piece of glass which is reflecting the sun.

31. Long shot. The right-hand side of the screen is filled by a tree trunk. The boy falls off his bike.

32. Sutherland looks up from the light-box.

33. 'A-ha!' Christie, reading from a book: 'Lake Ontario curves more than three degrees from its easternmost shore to . . .'

34. Christie: '. . . its westernmost shore . . .' Sutherland stands up. A stained-glass window can be seen behind him. Christie: '. . . so frozen water isn't flat.' He starts walking and looks back hurriedly: 'Nothing is what . . .'

35. Sutherland: '. . . it seems.' (It is typical of Roeg that he should hide the key to the film in such a throwaway remark.) Christie is sitting on a chesterfield: 'My cigarettes.' She moves as though about to get up.

36. Sutherland, standing: 'Did you put all the, er, window slides together?'

37. Christie looks round. The right-hand third of the shot is taken up by the blank projector screen. She points: 'No. I put the duplicates in my tray.' She puts her fingers to her mouth.

38. Christine with her fingers to her mouth. This physical similarity between mother and daughter echoes a line in du Maurier's story when 'Laura, her mouth set sulkily' reminds John 'instantly, with a pang, of their poor lost child' (p. 25). The tin hat is back on the Action Man's head. Christine is looking at something and smiling.

39. Same set-up as shot 37. Christie, searching for her smokes, lifts up a sofa cushion.

40. Close-up of the kitchen table. Plates piled high with the debris of Sunday lunch. A cigarette smoulders in an ashtray. Silence.

41. Christie continues her search.

42. Head-shot of Sutherland looking into the middle distance. His enigmatic expression could be one of love for his wife or one of puzzlement. Has he heard or seen something?

43. The boy examines the tyre on the front wheel of his upturned bike. The pond and the house are in the background. 'Action Man patrol . . .'

44. '. . . fall in.' He turns to look at his sister in the distance. She is by the water's edge and about to follow the order all too literally. 'Enemy in sight.'

45. Sutherland, slide in hand, walks over to the desk. He leans over to pick up a pack of cigarettes. He shakes it.

46. Christine, ball in hand, doll in the other, stands by the water. She throws the ball.

47. Christie catches the cigarettes. She smiles. Sutherland walks towards her, catching the leg of the desk: 'Oh shit . . .' We hear the sound of a glass tipping over.

48. The ball lands in the water. Plop.

49. Close-up of the overturned glass on the light-box.

The camera pulls back as if recoiling from the accident. The tumbler rolls into perfect horizontal alignment with the magnifying glass and the slide. Was it an accident?

50. Sutherland mops up the spilled water.

51. The red and white ball spins on the surface of the pond.

52. The boy extracts a piece of broken glass from the tyre with a pair of pliers.

53. Sutherland examines the slide through the magnifying glass. The camera moves so that it can see through it as well.

54. Close-up of the slide. Red starts to spread from the hooded figure. It snakes across the slide from right to left.

55. Sutherland gazes down at it. He raises his head and looks into the middle distance.

56. Long shot. The boy comes running round the pond.

57. Sutherland still looking into the middle distance. 'What's the matter?' asks Christie, still reading on the sofa. Sutherland disappears behind the screen then comes back into shot: 'Nothing.' He leaves the room. Christie looks after him. She picks up a slide.

58. A cross fills the shot. We are looking through the frame of a four-paned window in the white kitchen door. Sutherland comes through it. Footsteps. He runs out of the back door.

59. Christine, flat on her back, sinks below the surface of the pond.

60. Sutherland comes round a corner of the house.

61. Christine continues sinking.

62. Long shot. The boy continues running: 'Dad!'

63. Long shot. Sutherland runs towards the pond. 'Dad!'

64. Low-angle shot. The ball is on the pond in the foreground. The boy runs towards his father and stops at his feet as he leaps down the bank. Cut on the leap.

65. Sutherland lands. A perfect jump-cut. The boy, leaning against the bank, looks back. Sutherland keeps on running.

66. Front view (presumably from a boat). He steps into the water. Splash.

67. Side view. He wades towards the ball. Does the icy water makes him gasp or is it horror?

68. Close-up of the boy. He is playing with the piece of glass he extracted from the tyre.

69. Side view. Sutherland struggles through the water.

70. Front view. The ball is in the foreground. He takes a deep breath.

71. Christie examines a slide on the sofa.

72. Sutherland stares at the surface of the pond. Why is he hesitating?

73. Christie looks at the slide.

74. The blood-red continues to spread across the slide on the light-box.

75. Sutherland braces himself and plunges below the surface of the water.

76. Christie puts down the slide on a book *Beyond the Fragile Geometry of Space*. Its author is John Baxter. A roaring sound begins. Is this the blood rushing in John's ears? Is the fragile structure of his family now a thing of the past?

77. The red forms a foetal shape on the slide. A terrible evil is born. Cellos start moaning on the soundtrack. Dissolve.

78. Slow motion. John Baxter emerges from beneath the water clutching Christine.

79. A second angle. John emerges from the water again.

80. A third angle – marked once again by a separate chord on the soundtrack. John emerges from the water.

81. Close-up of John's hands round Christine. The waterproof coat could not save her.

82. Repeat of shot 80. John howls.

83. Close-up of Christine in her father's arms.

84. Dissolve to the slide. An eye has developed in the foetus as it continues to grow. It forms exactly the same shape as the drowned Christine (and Wendy's mermaid brooch).

85. Dissolve to Christine in her father's arms. He howls silently. His breath is steaming, the water streaming. He turns towards the house.

86. The surface of the pond. John exits the shot on the right. Christine's trailing, red-stockinged feet have lost their wellingtons. Harp glissandi.

87. Dissolve. Water continues to spread round the red foetus on the slide. It turns blue then white and stops. A thunderous clanking grows louder on the soundtrack.

88. Side view. Normal speed. John gives Christine the kiss of life by the water's edge.

89. Front view – i.e. the point of view of the boy. His father gives his sister the kiss of life.

90. The boy is still playing with the piece of glass. He sucks the little finger of his right hand. The raucous rooks continue to caw.

91. Front view. John continues to try and revive his daughter. The mud squelches. Water trickles off them.

92. Side view. He realises that it is no use. He cradles her bedraggled head in his arms. There is pondweed in her hair.

93. Front view. He gasps in horror and hugs her. He begins to lift her up.

94. Side view. Hand-held camera. John picks up Christine and moans.

95. Front view. He starts to carry her back to the house, moaning. He slips in the mud and topples onto his back but does not let go of his daughter.

96. Reaction-shot of the boy who is still fiddling with the shard of glass.

97. Through the kitchen window from the outside. Christie walks into the room with a cigarette.

98. John wrestles with Christine in the mud. He picks her up once again and continues to moan. He turns to the house on his knees.

99. Through the kitchen window. Christie moves from left to right. There are red flowers behind her.

100. John gets to his feet and staggers towards the house.

101. Christie comes out, turns and screams. Her fingers fly to her mouth as in shot 37.

102. Jump-cut to the power-drill driving into the stone of St Nicholas's, Venice.

It is a devastating sequence, its impact increased for being so compact. Roeg has thrown a rock into the pond and the rest of the film simply watches the ripples spread out. How the Baxters react to the repercussions of the tragedy provides the storyline, but the viewer, too, has been plunged into a pool of startling images and is faced with the task of how to make sense of this sensory overload.

With the benefit of hindsight it is possible to pick out all the clues but an audience seeing the film for the first time does not have this luxury. It is only when the experience is repeated that they, like John Baxter, can call on second sight to help them.

The remainder of the picture expands and partially explains the significance of the opening sequence. Christine's crossing the wooden bridge is mirrored time and again by her parents as they cross and recross bridges – both material and metaphorical – in Venice. This sense of being on the threshold is given added weight by a preponderance of doors and windows which is sustained throughout *Don't Look Now*. John goes through three doors to get to Christine. He goes through a lot more to get to the dwarf. Laura is often viewed through a window: she will soon be a widow. The building itself – half wood, half brick, half old, half new – is neither one thing nor the other. A halfway house is the ideal home for people who are in two minds about something.

Laura keeps her daughter's red and white ball in her suitcase. When a person dies their possessions are imbued with an extra value; the objects are as close as you can get to the person. In Venice a little boy plays with an identical ball in hospital. The idea of 'duplicates' – whether slides, toys or doppelgangers – is played with throughout the film. Are we seeing the real thing or is it a copy? Laura, discussing his father's work, tells Johnny that, 'I can't tell the difference between his repaired windows and the originals.' John judges the Scottish sisters to be fakes. Laura thinks they are genuine. The audience is left to make up its own mind.

The shot of Christine's reflection in the water as she runs alongside it recurs again and again. Water kills her and gives birth to the evil embryo on the slide. The fact that they are both red unites them instantly and permanently but it is Christine's reflection or mirror image that represents the dwarf, not the girl herself. The inversion shows that the woman in red is the opposite of the child whose name means a follower of Christ: a withered limb of Satan.

The drowning is foreshadowed by John's knocking over a glass of water. A glass of water is such a simple thing, usually offered as an aid to recovery, but in *Don't Look Now* it is associated with disaster. When we see Johnny after his accident at school, a glass of water is prominently displayed on his bedside table. When the Baxters have their furious row – 'Christine is dead. She is dead – dead, dead, dead, dead, dead' – John gives Laura a glass of water but she deceives him and does not take her tranquilliser. Thereafter husband and wife are on separate tracks. And, shortly before his confrontation with the dwarf, John asks for a glass of water in the sisters' hotel room. Glass is a visual paradox, a supercooled liquid that appears to be solid. It is both firm and brittle. It can let in light yet its invisibility can be dangerous. Johnny's bike smashes a pane of glass; John in his death throes kicks out a fanlight. In every sense the film is a shattering experience.

A glass of water combines fluidity with fragility; Roeg's technique reflects this. His fluid camerawork – the tracking of people and vehicles; shot after shot of flowing water – creates a restless atmosphere of perpetual motion which is occasionally broken up by deliberate fragmentation: jagged editing and fractured time. If the long shots and low angles provoke a sense of unease in the viewer, and the camera appears to be playing hide-and-seek, jump-cuts can make you jump.

When the father blows his brains out in *Walkabout* we see him fall back against the black Beetle three times from three different angles. When John bursts out of the water with Christine in slow motion – which emphasises his sodden heaviness – we see him do so three times from three different angles. In moments of extreme stress time does seem to stagger, if not actually stand still. One's state of awareness is so heightened that the mind is unable to deal with the sudden surge in stimuli and appears to slow down. Every detail of the experience is making a conscious impression so that time seems to stretch. Roeg forces the spectator to share in the protagonist's trauma, to identify more closely with John Baxter so that his horror is all the more harrowing. In a similar way, when the plank falls onto the cradle as John inspects the mosaic in St Nicholas's – smashing a glass screen on which various pictures, transparencies and photographs have been stuck – Roeg stretches the moment so that the viewer is given enough time to ask 'Did I see something out of the corner of my eye or not?' before providing the upsetting answer.

But the dislocation of time is not always negative. The sex scene, intercut with shots of John and Laura dressing after the event, is unmistakably positive. So is the build up to it. Their shouted conversation between bathroom and bedroom ('you heard me that time'); John considering his love-handles; the maid surprising him in the nude (don't look now); Laura telling him he has toothpaste around his mouth, all contribute to the atmosphere of warm, fond and long-established intimacy. Skilful editing transforms what could have been just another bonk into a scene of lyrical love-making. Its afterglow – witnessed as the couple prepare to go out for dinner – spreads into the following scenes and is only dispersed by the scream of the serial killer's victim. The scene gains in poignancy when we realise that the Baxters will never be as close again.

The prologue sketches a picture of domestic bliss – parents relaxing after a blow-out lunch while the children play in the garden – only so that it can be immediately demolished. We are made aware of how much is being lost. The nuclear family approaches meltdown. Christine's watery reflection is followed by an image of her mother by the fire. Laura is in her element: she is the one who lights the candles for Christine, she is the one who initiates the love-making. Whereas John is ruled by the head, she is ruled by the heart. Father and daughter are identified with red, the colour of blood, danger, martyrdom and magic; mother and son seen in shades of blue, the traditional colour of hope, loyalty and faith. But *Don't Look Now* does not adhere to a strict symbolic code. The colours are used impressionistically to enhance mood, not for their intrinsic meaning.

Nevertheless the audience is faced with a dilemma: do they, along with John, see red or, along with Laura, feel blue? Anger and depression are two of the main manifestations of grief. Red is the dominant colour in John's scarf, the colour of a sweater hanging upside down over a canal (like the corpse that will soon be fished out of it), a dressing-gown, a bobble-hat, the blanket on Johnny's bed, a candle, carpet and the glass on the bishop's mantelpiece that holds the night-light he stares at as John meets his bloody end. When John sees his funeral in flash-forward Pino Donnagio's superb score bursts into a Vivaldi-like frenzy. Vivaldi, a native Venetian, was nicknamed 'The Red Priest'. Are these significant or mere red herrings? Blue is the colour of a policeman's flashing light and the main colour of the tiles in the mosaic. The eye is forever being caught by a splash of colour that stands out all the more against the

John and Laura share an intimate meal in Venice.

muted tones of Venice. Like the characters themselves, we are forced to be on the lookout, never sure which way to turn.

Cinema is the art of *trompe l'oeil* which, according to *Chambers Dictionary*, is 'literally "something that deceives the eye"; appearance of reality achieved by use of minute, often trivial, details or of other effects in painting, architecture, etc.' For instance, the walls of Johnny's headmaster's study appear to be hung with paintings but they are not: the pictures are part of a wallpaper design. The gradual accumulation of illustrated books, slides, pictures, windows and glass of various kinds invites us to not only reflect on them but also to see through them, to be conscious of the fact that we are looking at a visual construct.

Many of these self-referents can be glimpsed in the opening sequence. Black comedy is present in the Action Man's order to 'fall in', John's assurance that 'nothing' is wrong, in the savage destruction of the postprandial idyll. Gothic is there in the ominous presence of the rooks, the curious house and a creeping sense of unease. But none of these is allowed to detract from its emotional charge: whether seeing it for the first or fifteenth time the overwhelming impression is of sudden, inexplicable tragedy followed by numbed disbelief. Any death is a terrible event but the death of a child is especially horrifying. No parent should have to outlive their offspring. And Roeg, during the rest of the film, makes us relive the shock over and over again.

6 'It's incredible you can't change your course.'

Black comedy views life as a series of misfortunes occasionally relieved by the misfortunes of others. Banana skins, pratfalls, last-minute hitches – the many slips twixt lip and cup – all go to show that, no matter how hard we try or how high we aim, we are doomed to come a cropper. The good life – those rare moments when everything seems to be going just right – turns out to be a mere respite from the usual bad timing.

The Baxters, devotees of *la dolce vita*, are totally unprepared – mentally and physically – to deal with disaster. *Don't Look Now* gives them a brutal baptism in reality: Christine drowns, Laura breaks down, Johnny is injured and John is murdered. No one can bear too much reality and it is the unbearableness of their story that transmutes the comedy into tragedy.

After the shocking opening the film swiftly declutches and the pace slows down so that the tension can be gradually increased once more. The shift to gentle comedy invites the viewer to relax but already the outlines of the filmic mosaic have been drawn and, in some ways, it is just a question of putting in the pieces one by one, colour by colour.

The jump-cut from Laura's scream to the power-drill covers a change in location as well as a lapse in time. Christine's death, her funeral and the flight to Italy are thus immediately consigned to history. The mourning, though, continues. John seeks solace in his work which attempts to undo the ravages of the past, to make something good out of the bad. He forgets the time: he is late for lunch with Laura whom we see writing a letter to Johnny. She has more success in communicating with her son than her husband. When John asks if he should add a few lines, Laura tells him to write his own letter. But he never gives himself the chance: he is too preoccupied with his job. He keeps saying that he must take some time off but he does not even do so when Johnny is hurt – a fatal mistake. The point is emphasised by the bishop when he admonishes him 'you should have gone'. Advice, premonitions and warnings have no effect on John: he is deaf to his own death. He will neither see nor speak to his son again. Nowadays it would be said that John is 'in denial': refusing to face up to unpalatable truths. By turning his attention to the peculiar properties of stone, the qualities of glass and the interaction of air and water on them, John – like the father (John Meillon) in *Walkabout* who studies the paper on structural geology shortly before shooting himself – can block out the blackness. But only for so long.

It is his attempt to shut out the draught – 'it's so cold in here the waiters don't come' – that precipitates the Big Chill. The simple action of closing the window by their table blows open the french windows across the room and sends a piece of grit into Wendy's eye, thus providing the pretext for Laura to go to her aid. The moment is even accompanied by a fanfare of doom: a vaporetto sounds its horn as the doors blast open. When Laura returns with her good tidings John is still so wrapped up in his project – 'the mastic that works is number three' – he does not see that she is going to faint: she falls onto the table bringing everything crashing to the marble floor. Olive oil is poured on troubled waters: but nothing – glass, plate, or bone – is broken.

Christine falls into the pond, Johnny falls off his bike, John – with his daughter in his arms – falls in the mud, Laura drops in a dead faint, John almost falls to his death in St Nicholas's and the bishop tells John that his father died in a fall. None of this is intrinsically funny – it is sick rather than slapstick – but it all goes towards creating an atmosphere in which if anything can go wrong it will. Likewise the lack of communication between husband and wife. There is no doubt that John and Laura love each other. John tries to protect Laura from what he sees as the sisters' unhealthy, not to say unholy, influence. He fails. Laura, having misinterpreted the prophecy, then tries to save him from its fulfilment. She fails. That such marital misunderstandings can be comic is demonstrated by the headmaster and his wife. The scene in which Anthony Babbage calls the Baxters in the middle of the night – 'Hal-lo . . . Hal-lo . . . Hal-lo . . .' – but has to be rescued by his spouse Mandy (Ann Rye) perfectly captures the air of embarrassed inarticulacy.

There are no crossed wires but it takes an unconscionable time to get the message across. Very British. The book on John's bedside table by the telephone, *Der Stellvertreter* by Rolf Hochhuth, is a play about the Roman Catholic Church's alleged complicity with Fascism and concerns the so-called Nazi Pope, Pius XII. 'I went to a great deal of trouble to get *The Representative* in Italy,' Roeg explained to me, 'but I was told it was unacceptable. In the end I thought "bollocks!" – John can read it in the original German instead.'

The first scene in Venice establishes that John can speak Italian but that in moments of stress – trying to find Laura in the sisters' hotel, trying to find the sisters themselves – this ability vanishes. The fact that Renato Scarpa who plays Inspector Longhi cannot speak English very well – indeed he had no idea what he was saying – makes the character

The sinister Inspector Longhi (Renato Scarpa).

all the more sinister. When John first enters his office the cop's face is entirely hidden by a lamp on his desk. He pops out from behind it: 'Hallo!' It is as if he is playing peekaboo. His cute baby-face features and diminutive size – emphasised when he stands alongside Sutherland – do not inspire confidence in his powers of detection. The politeness with which his remarks are made only heighten their bizarre content: 'The skill of police artists is to make the living appear dead.' When he puts down the impressions of the sisters we glimpse a black-and-white picture of a corpse. Something horrid has been done to the eyes. Meanwhile, through the window, he watches the sisters, arm-in-arm, stroll innocently past. There is no sign of Laura. When the inspector toys with the crumpled photograph of her all that can be seen of the *Il Gazzettino* masthead is 'IL'. Is she ill, suffering a relapse or just being bamboozled by the sisters? John came to the police for help. He – and we – leave with added hindrance.

The other minor characters are equally disturbing. Even the female

The enigmatic Bishop Barbarrigò (Massimo Serrato).

turnkey, who has been guarding Heather after her arrest, gives a ridiculous twitchy smile as she watches her leave with John. Why? The hotel manager (played by Italian film critic Leopoldo Trieste) is a Basil Fawlty figure who cannot wait to be rid of his guests. He is helpful enough in finding Laura a seat on a charter flight going out of the country but when John later returns to ask if he has seen her – interrupting a dalliance with a whispering chambermaid – he turns sulky and menacing, fingering a comb as if it were a switchblade and forcing him to back out of his office. A similar moment occurs during the initial encounter with the bishop when he meets Laura: 'A woman to share your sins with . . .' Clearly he is no ordinary priest. As he walks along he suddenly opens his coat and, for a split-second, it seems that, like some mafioso, he is about to pull out a gun, but he is only retrieving his handkerchief. By bombarding the viewer with a kaleidoscope of images Roeg constantly forces us into the position of having to decide – instantly – whether a particular close-up is significant or irrelevant, part of the overall pattern or mere background. He makes nervous wrecks of us all so that we identify with John's predicament: neither of us know where to look.

Bishop Barbarrigo continues to be an enigma. He believes that 'we have stopped listening' to God but John – who certainly has deaf ears – believes that the bishop 'doesn't give an ecclesiastical fuck' about the restoration of St Nicholas's. One minute he is boasting that the suppliers of the mosaic tiles have been making tesserae for his family for over two hundred years, the next – after the cradle falls away from John and a scaffolding pole nearly crowns the cleric – he is crunching them underfoot. If God treats those who care for his houses in such a cavalier fashion, God help those who do not care for him. But as the religious paraphernalia – crucifixes, candles, relics and regalia – accumulates it is drained of meaning; powerless to prevent evil, the Church is reduced to just another system of ritualised superstition. Sometimes it works, sometimes it does not. When Laura escapes injury after fainting she considers it to be a miracle – and the Baxters cross and recross the

Bridge of Miracles – but John tells her that 'the unconscious body reacts faster than the mind ever can' and the slow-motion stresses this. Heather's miraculous powers, witnessed during the seance, merely provide a different kind of service.

The specificity of these two characters makes them both funnier and more feasible. This is mainly due to their Scottishness: 'She's quite famous round Elgin,' says Wendy of her sister, proudly; and, when John brings Heather back to the hotel, Wendy, told to offer him a whisky, reluctantly admits. 'There's the miniatures we got for Jessie' (which contain Scotch of course). Wendy, in a series of silly hats, is the butch bossy-boots; years of looking after her sister have made her long-suffering and short-tempered. Heather, in contrast, is more polite (probably because she often has to rely on the kindness of strangers) and less down-to-earth. Deprived of sight, she lives in her imagination where she may or may not see things. What is not in doubt is that both women feel things: Wendy can sympathise with Laura because she, too, has lost a child. The ambiguous nature of their relationship is amusing but there are times when they are treated with what can only be described as cruelty. When Wendy upbraids Heather for wearing odd-coloured socks (even though she put them out for her), it is impossible not to giggle. This may be mocking the afflicted but callousness is an essential part of black comedy. Everyone is fair game. This is hell and we are all in it together.

Such vindictiveness may spring from a resentment of Heather's psychic ability which gives the sisters a baleful hold over us. Laura – and we – need her to reassure us. Laura is desperate to get in touch with Christine. Is her daughter really happy? We need to know if she is genuine – and therefore worthy of our attention and respect – or a fake, in which case – if there is no afterlife after all – we can continue to laugh at her with impunity. It is the not knowing that makes us afraid. Their potential for duplicity puts us in two minds about them.

Once John has been killed and the prophecy apparently fulfilled Laura has no need of Heather: she marches off the funeral barge to the

7 'Nothing can take the place of the one that's gone.'

When someone you love dies a part of you dies with them. You see the world through different eyes – not those of a man who receives a last-minute reprieve on his way to the gas chamber and finds new joy in the fact of his very being but those of someone finally robbed of their rose-tinted spectacles. Or, to put it another way, a life lived in Technicolor CinemaScope is suddenly reduced to black-and-white Video 8. All colour and meaning drain away. How do you go on without them?

There are no easy answers – and *Don't Look Now* does not offer any – but various strategies are suggested. The conventional response is to turn to God. Bishop Barbarrigo is an unconventional priest but remains within the Church. He is a believer: 'I wish I didn't have to believe in prophecy. I do – but I wish I didn't have to.' As John dies Barbarrigo wakes up in his chaste single bed and, like a lost little boy, looks to a picture of the Good Shepherd for comfort. The last John and we see of him is a flashback of him standing in St Nicholas's – gazing up at John as he dangles from the broken cradle – a frightened and lonely man.

When Inspector Longhi has finished listening to John's story he could be speaking for all of us when he says: 'There must be more.' He has not been given the full story. Neither has anybody else. The idea that an eternal, paternal figure is looking down on us benevolently (even if he does not manage to look *after* us) is a consolation to some. Mary Lou (Candy Clark) in *The Man Who Fell to Earth* puts it this way: 'When you look out there at night, don't you feel that somewhere there's gotta be a God? There's gotta be!'

Heather has no trouble in reconciling her psychic powers with her strong Scottish faith: 'Second sight is a gift from the good Lord, who sees all things; and I consider it an impertinence to call his creatures back from rest for our entertainment.' She, too, has suffered loss – that of her nephew, her sister's son. 'It jars you losing one like that,' says Wendy.

The bond between Laura and the sisters can be partly attributed to this shared experience: the older women know what Laura is going through. There is also a maternal aspect to their relationship. When Wendy first meets Laura she tells her: 'Goodness, you do remind me of my daughter.' She points out that Laura can always have another child. Indeed, after the love-making of the previous evening, she may already be pregnant. Whether or not the sisters are phonies, their friendship is genuine. And they undoubtedly succeed in helping Laura. John cannot accept this. Laura tries to explain – 'Listen. I've been trying very hard to hang on to myself and to forget about what happened, get rid of this emptiness that's been with me like some pain' – but John will not see her point of view. It is almost as if he were jealous of them. They seem to be able to help his wife, to stop her having a breakdown, whereas he

Laura forms a bond with the two sisters (Hilary Mason and Clelia Matania).

cannot, and this increases his sense of impotence. He could not save his daughter's life and now his marriage seems in jeopardy.

Guilt is often felt following bereavement – even if not directly to blame, your inability to prevent the death still rankles – and the simple fact that you go on living while your loved one does not can be enough to create a sense of being in the wrong. Laura does not pull her punches. She reminds John that he should have been keeping an eye on Christine: 'You let her go near that pond . . . You said you'd give your life in exchange for hers, well you can't do that . . . John, she's trying to get in touch with us, maybe to forgive . . .' It is an incredibly cruel thing to say. It reveals Laura's desperation and determination to believe in Heather's powers, her need to know that Christine is all right.

Any marriage would be put under strain in such circumstances but for John – battling with his own grief and self-recriminations – the accusation is too much to bear and he pushes Laura away, shoving her in the direction of the sisters' hotel: 'Go on, you crazy woman.' She can go her way and he will go his. It is an ugly moment in a movie packed with tender ones and therefore all the more shocking.

Up until this point it is the togetherness of the Baxters that is emphasised. Roeg does this in the simplest and most economical of ways: he shows John and Laura holding hands. In the restaurant John holds Laura's hand and says 'I must take some time off' but, being a workaholic, he does not and ends up paying the price. There is no doubt that he would give his life in exchange for Christine's but his ultimate sacrifice – intended or not – is more penance than recompense and only seems to confirm the presence of the afterlife. When Laura is carried out to the water-ambulance John holds her hand. When he comes to collect her from the hospital he holds both her hands in both of his. When they walk together, they do so arm-in-arm. Even when apart they are linked by a common gesture: a shot of Laura holding a glass of whisky at the seance is followed by one of John holding his glass in the nearby bar. *Don't Look Now* is an intensely romantic movie. The Baxters love each other deeply but love is just as useless in the face of death as anything else. When the row is finally concluded in their hotel bedroom, and Laura merely pretends to take a pill, the scene ends with a close-up of her holding her own hands.

Holding hands with someone is both a physical and figurative act. Parents hold their children's hands to guide them and give them security. A nurse holds a patient's hand to comfort them. Lovers hold hands to feel the warmth of each other's flesh and to tell the world that the two of them are one. It is the plainest demonstration of only connecting. To see it, to do it, is touching.

Heather, unable to use her eyes, has to rely on touch more than most. The sisters are shown holding hands at the start of the film when Laura helps them to the ladies'. Once they know where they are their hands separate. A close-up emphasises that the connection has been broken and, sure enough, they proceed to bicker about the best way to remove the grit in Wendy's eye. But, at the end of the film, they process into St Nicholas's for John's funeral arm-in-arm: their relationship remains unscathed.

Don't Look Now begins and ends with violent separations. In its beginning lies its end: the drowning of Christine and the spawning of the red homunculus sow the seeds of John's own destruction. The worst aspect of bereavement is the absence: like an amputee you can sense the missing part of you. In a way, the bereft are victims of a serial killer: they have to learn over and over again that their loved one is, in John's words, 'dead, dead, dead, dead, dead, dead'. As the amputee feels the unfeelable, the bereaved see the unseeable. They are haunted.

John's initial reaction to what he sees as a little girl in red is one of fear and incredulity: he cannot believe his own eyes. And yet, only hours before in the hospital, he tells Laura: 'Seeing is believing.' He turns his back on the vision, rejoins his wife, and returns to 'the real world'. 'What on earth was that?' asks Laura, referring to the blood-curdling cry. Shaken and confused, all he can come up with is 'a cat'. Neither they nor we are convinced.

When she accuses him of causing Christine's death John replies –

half in anger, half in anguish – 'Thanks for the memories, Laura.'
Ghosts are memories that materialise: guests that are both wanted and
unwanted. John is a rationalist but there are no rational explanations
for ghosts, only emotional ones. He is constantly being reminded of
Christine: the children in hospital, the doll he salvages from the canal.
As he continues to see red, his suspicion that he might have second sight
becomes all the more difficult to deny, as Heather says, 'It's a curse as
well as a gift.' Part of him, the heart of him, must ache to be reunited
with his daughter but another part of him, his head, refuses to
countenance the possibility of life after death, even though he spends his
working life preserving monuments to such a belief. If seeing things is a
sign of insanity, John has every right to be mad with grief.

　　Memories by their very nature are historical but the human

'The Baxters love
each other deeply
but love is just as
useless in the face
of death as
anything else.'

memory does not work chronologically. It keeps time in a pool of associations, emotions and impressions that can be dipped into anyhow and anywhere. When an object of your affections is summarily removed all that is left is the memory of them and it is truly astonishing what can be remembered. In recalling often long-forgotten details – something they once said, a certain laugh, the feel of their hair in your fingers – it is as if the mind is deliberately reconstructing the lost person, creating a mental replica of them. The wealth of material it has unconsciously recorded about them can be frightening. You reach the stage where it seems they have been virtually living in your head. Which, in a sense, they have. We are all prisoners of our own and others' perceptions.

But it is not enough. An image, no matter how good, is not the same as the real thing. There has to be some concrete proof that they lived, that they are not just a figment of the imagination after all. Photographs, whether professional portraits or just holiday snaps, immediately become priceless. They are something to hold on to and, by enabling you to relive the pain, perhaps they can eventually relieve it.

If photographs are memories that have been printed out then both are examples of *déjà vu*. The red dwarf is seen by John time and again – always on the other side of the water – but he and we are tricked into thinking that we have seen her before – in the guise of Christine – the very first time we see her. We are not allowed to see through her disguise. In other words we have been inside John's head from the very beginning. Memory – ever with us but never under our control – can ambush us at any time in any place and Roeg makes the most of this. While Laura is helping the sisters in the ladies', John recalls the recent nightmare but although we witness the Baxters' rain-swept departure through his eyes we come out of the memory through Heather's unseeing eyes: John's hindsight merges with her second sight in a timeless present. Heather may be on the same wavelength as John and thus be able to pick up his thoughts; she may have tuned in to Laura's grief; how she gained her impressions does not matter. What counts is the fact that what she says is true: Christine did have 'light hair, silky soft'; she was wearing 'a shiny little mac'. Whether this is good guesswork or rare intuition it is sufficiently impressive to make her words tantalisingly plausible: 'You're sad. You're so sad. And there's no need to be.' If only she were right.

The little black bust of Angus and the collection of family photographs are clearly precious to both sisters. When John brings Heather back to their new hotel she asks Wendy: 'Have you put the photos out?' At the seance Wendy is not very pleased when she realises that Laura has been touching them: 'Was that Angus?' she asks sharply. The mementos are treated with a reverance normally afforded holy relics and, in a way, that is exactly what they are.

The perpetual cloud of doubt hanging over Heather and Wendy complicates our response to them and offers scant consolation. We never do find out if Christine is happy nor do we discover any evidence that we shall all live happily in the hereafter. Laura is convinced of their authenticity early on but at the same time she is portrayed as the weaker partner in the marriage: she is the one who suffered a breakdown. After her fall, though, she recovers from her fainting fit and goes from strength to strength. John, on the other hand, dismisses them out of hand and continues with his work but he is soon seeing things and throwing up, his body refusing to act on the warnings issued by his disturbed mind.

When John climbs the scaffold to examine the mosaic high up in St Nicholas's we see Wendy's face in a halo of light; he nearly dies. When John climbs the spiral staircase to his death Heather's face appears in the same way. Both have been called cheat shots. But why? We are inside John's head and it is only natural that dangerous situations should bring her doomy prophecy to mind. They are memories and as such may even partly explain what happens next: you only have to tell someone perched on a ledge not to look down for them to immediately do so. Don't look now. The past plays on the present to produce the future. Just as the future impinges on the present while the Baxters make love – 'ecstasy' comes from the Greek words meaning to stand out from: from the body, from time – so his future death impinges on the present. After Laura has flown out of Venice he sees her and the sisters glide past his *vaporetto*. He is so surprised he does not realise what kind of boat it is – a funeral barge, his funeral barge.

John's overwrought mind is not only playing tricks on him, it is telling him – if only he would see – what will happen if he ignores his own intuition. On a physical level his subsequent demise is the result of basic cause and effect: John is in mourning, working too hard, separated from his wife and preoccupied by the promptings of the sisters and his own sixth sense. He cannot think straight, makes a foolish error, mistakes a dwarf for his daughter and dies, the innocent victim of a serial killer. On a psychological level it also makes sense: John, terminally exhausted, is overwhelmed by guilt, anger and grief, and, half

Laura and the sisters glide past.

in love with easeful death, rushes on to meet his fate. There are times when oblivion has its own attractions. Nietzsche, not the most reliable of moral guides admittedly, confessed in Chapter Four of *Beyond Good and Evil*: 'The thought of suicide is a great source of comfort.' If you cannot bring the loved one back, then why not go on and join them?

If Roeg is holding a mirror up to Nietzsche it is possible to interpret the reflections in different ways. Likewise with Heather's prophecy. John, in turning a blind eye to it, ensures its realisation. Laura, who does believe in the sisters, mistakes its subject – it is John not Johnny who is in danger (perhaps this explains why father and son have the same name) – but she both survives and is revived by her leap of faith. When we first see her in Venice she is so low she cannot even be bothered to order a meal: 'I'll have what I had last night.' At the close she is walking tall with her son and smiling – even though she is attending the funeral of her husband. And we are left in no doubt that she knows what John is running after and what is about to happen to him. The last we see of her before the murder is her reaching through the locked iron gate, trying to connect with John *and* Christine: 'Darlings!' What follows would be enough to send anyone over the brink.

'John, terminally exhausted … rushes on to meet his fate.'

8 'We're almost there.'

Don't Look Now is not a Hollywood movie but it follows one of its favourite formulae to the letter: tell the audience what they are going to see, show it them and then tell them what they have seen. The opening sequence sets the parameters of the action, the main body of the film fills in the outlines, and the closing sequence – the last seconds of John Baxter's life – reviews the story and, with a flourish, casts a whole new light on it. Roeg is like a master magician who begins his act with an amazing trick but, for the finale, pulls off the same trick in a fraction of the original time. If you thought the start of *Don't Look Now* was startling, you ain't seen nothing yet.

The prelude to the final confrontation is strangely faithful to du Maurier's story: the 'bolt which he rammed into its socket' (p. 54) – keeping out John's rescuer not the dwarf's attacker – becomes the lock that he turns to keep the iron gates closed. Similarly, to meet his nemesis, he has to climb 'another flight of stairs, which were spiral, twisting, leading to the floor above'. The shape of them is mirrored in the vortices of the swirling fog, lurking just above the floor of the derelict *palazzo*, which is disturbed by the footsteps of the dwarf and then by John himself. It is a suitably Gothic touch which enhances the chase through a succession of empty doorways: his persistent fog of incomprehension will clear as he crosses the final threshold. The audience sees the light as John does and Roeg's rapid editing ensures that it comes in a blaze of emotion.

1. John smiles at the dwarf huddling in the corner.
2. John sees the slide with the red foetal shape – as in shot 84 of the opening sequence – and his smile vanishes. We hear the four flute notes that introduced the dwarf in shot 26.
3. The dwarf turns round and waddles towards him. We can hear her breathing heavily. A roaring, clanking sound begins.
4. John's reaction to the hideous sight. The camera, adopting the

dwarf's point of view, comes closer and closer. John: 'Wait.'

5. The dwarf turns her hooded head from side to side, as if saying 'no'.

6. The bishop's head turns from left to right on his pillow. He sits up. The camera pulls back. He looks at the candle in the red glass on the mantelpiece.

7. The camera zooms in on Heather who is standing in one of the arches in her bedroom. She begins to scream: 'No!'

8. John: 'Wait!' The scream continues.

9. The dwarf continues to turn her head from side to side. The camera follows her hand to her right pocket. She pulls out a knife.

10. Johnny comes running round the pond – as in shot 56 of the opening sequence. (Henceforth indicated by the number in brackets.)

The dwarf-murderess (Adelina Poerio) prowls the alleyways and backstreets.

11. John wrestles with the gargoyle. Stone grinds against stone.

12. The dwarf hacks the left side of John's neck.

13. Close-up of the blade sinking into his flesh. Crunch. Church bells ring out.

14. Laura screams (101).

15. Blood spurts from John's neck. He gasps and falls to the right.

16. John holds Christine in his arms (83).

17. The ball lands on the pond (48).

18. Close-up of the knife in John's neck. He falls away, gasping.

19. Johnny in bed after his accident at school. There is a glass of water by his bedside, a red blanket over him, a red mark on his forehead. He begins to turn in his sleep.

20. The dwarf turns as in shot 3.

21. John hangs from the collapsing cradle.

22. The bishop looks up at him from the ground, the swinging camera increasing our sense of vertigo.

23. John on the ground in the *palazzo*. He begins to turn onto his back, blood spurting from his neck. He cries out.

24. Close-up of Christine. The piano music that introduced her at the start of the film begins. This time though it is assured, all trace of hesitation gone. This time though she is not smiling. Her odd expression could be one of fear, anger or frustration – as if she were saying, 'I told you so.'

25. Laura in the restaurant, the sisters behind her.

26. Close-up of John holding Laura's hand.

27. Close-up of Wendy's mermaid brooch.

28. John rolling on the ground *before* the blood has spilled.

29. Continuation of the zoom begun in shot 6. It comes to rest on Heather's milky blue eyes.

30. Close-up of her neck. Weird electronic noises.

31. Head-shot of John on the ground, blood pouring out of him.

32. John and Laura making love, writhing on the bed. John's mouth is open. Their piano theme swells.

33. John holds hands with Laura as she is carried out to the water-ambulance. She looks up at him.

34. Close-up of Laura smiling in hospital.

35. The blood continues to gush.

36. Inspector Longhi writing at his desk, the map of Venice behind him. He turns his head from side to side.

37. The dwarf brings out the knife as in shot 9.

38. Close-up of her turning head.

39. John falls and turns again.

40. The Baxters' first sight of the inspector. He is standing on the balcony at the murder scene where their boat reverses.

41. John emerges from the water holding Christine in his arms (78).

42. A female corpse is lowered into a police launch having been winched out of the canal.

43. Close-up of Laura's crumpled photograph in John's hands. He turns it over.

44. The sisters' collection of memorabilia: photos, bust, brooch and Johnnie Walker miniature.

45. The inspector puts the artist's impressions of the sisters on the photograph of the blinded corpse.

46. John rolls on the floor.

47. Laura lighting six candles.

48. Laura's ferry crosses the sparkling lagoon, seagulls wheeling and wailing.

49. Winter sunlight, filtering through bare trees, turns the pond into a mirror.

50. Laura sitting in the car in the rain. The camera pulls back.

51. Long shot. The car outside the Baxter's halfway house.

52. John on the floor goes into death throes.

53. His foot kicks out a fanlight in the room below. Breaking glass.

54. Johnny's front wheel smashes a pane of glass. The same sound of breaking glass.

55. John's foot kicks out the fanlight again. It continues to shake.

56. The camera whirls round the room below, revealing door after door after door.

57. John shuddering on the floor, his blood forming a pool on it.

58. The camera turns its attention to the ceiling of the room below which is decorated with an ornate circular design.

59. John's foot protrudes through the smashed fanlight. Blood trickles over the edge.

60. The spinning camera continues staring at the ceiling. John cannot be seeing this – he is in the room above. Has he already left his body? Is Heather seeing this?

61. Close-up of Heather's opaque blue eyes.

62. Dissolve to rain on the pond: the very first shot of the film.

63. Blood pours out of John as he writhes on the floor in agony.

64. Christine's reflection as she runs along the edge of the water.

65. Laura and the sisters glide past – right to left – on the funeral barge as seen in John's premonition. Wendy is wearing her brooch.

66. John, on the *vaporetto*, turns to look after them: 'Laura!'

67. John lies on the floor. There is blood on his chin. The piano music stops.

68. John's motionless foot protrudes through the broken fanlight. Blood streams down the wall.

69. Dissolve to the slide of the dwarf in St Nicholas's. The red spreads but this time the blurring goes further until it fills the whole screen, the colour vanishing in a white-out (rather like the final frame of *Two-Lane Blacktop* (1971) where the film appears to catch and melt in the projector). All the bells in Venice seem to toll John's death.

70. Jump-cut. John's floating funeral cortege – decked with red flowers that match his son's red cap – appears round the corner of a building. This time it moves from left to right: this time it is the real thing. All the characters stare defiantly ahead. There is no turning back now. A full orchestra – including organ – plays the main theme.

It is a superlative sequence – a milestone in modern cinema – which hits the viewer right between the eyes. It lasts less than two minutes but in that time Roeg achieves a number of things. First of all he is recapitulating in every sense of the word: going over the chief points of the story again; repeating stages of development in an embryo; and repeating earlier passages of a musical work. Not only *déjà vu* but also *déjà lu* and *déjà entendu*. Secondly, Roeg is showing us the final moments of a man's life in which past, present and future ebb back and forth until they are eventually swamped by death. Hence the splicing of flashbacks both distant and instant (i.e. the repetition of images only seconds old) with action that has yet to come. A drowning man is said to see his life pass before his eyes and, in a sense, John has been drowning ever since his daughter died. He hesitates before plunging his whole body into the

John's foretold funeral.

water (72) not because he has seen his reflection but because – whether through second sight or not – he recognises the reality of both Christine's death and his own. So Roeg has not just stretched John's dying agonies into two minutes – slowed time down so that we can appreciate every detail of it – he has expanded the first seven minutes of the film into a further 103. On one level, *Don't Look Now* is all over in the blink of an eye. Hence its title. The constant movement in each individual piece of the mini-mosaic – the turning, pouring and reeling – rehearses the action of the bigger picture which flows, runs, falls and rushes. One second is being smashed to smithereens. Speed is of the essence – a man is dying – and Roeg finds poetry in the motion. A tale about images, framing and cutting is told by images, framing and cutting.

Besides defining photography as 'truth twenty-four times a second', Jean-Luc Godard defined cinema as 'watching death at work'. John Baxter's death is unique but because it is viewed in the context of his living and loving it is one with which we can empathise. Death may be in store for us all but the cinema can only ever portray the ending of life – the rest is guesswork. So far no one – not even Walt Disney – has come back to share the experience. Ghosts represent our need to believe in some kind of continuity – even if the poor souls are stuck in limbo. And what are movie stars – who are said to have presence – if not professional ghosts? The flickering light of film, in showing us the after-images of fellow human beings, make us aware of the fleetingness of existence. The persistence of vision gives life to a series of still-lives. The best movies move not just physically but profoundly. *Don't Look Now* is a defiant demonstration of art's ability to make time stand still while acknowledging that everything – even the pain and grief of bereavement – must come to an end. If the living can never be with the dead, then maybe the dead are always with us. I hope so.

9 'I know where we are now.'

The following conversation took place in Roeg's book-lined study on the afternoon of Saturday 13 January 1996. His recollections were constantly interrupted by a tyrannical telephone, boisterous children, and a Jack Russell terrier called Gus. But none of this made any difference to his way of thinking: Prospero was in his cell.

What do you remember about the shoot?

Odd things happened with *Don't Look Now*. It ran very freely. It seemed impossible that Julie and Donald would be able to take part but, in the end, they came to the movie and they got into it right away, they just fell into it. After ten days Donald said: 'I'm just going to do what you say. It's the first time I've ever felt like this but it seems to be right, I feel comfortable in my part and I don't want to keep thinking about it. Where do we go next?' When that happens you're very lucky and it is difficult to keep on that course. I don't care for rehearsing and I've never used storyboards: if you have set things in mind you're immediately imposing yourself on the essence of the story and characters. I believe film has a life of its own but releasing yourself to it is by no means easy. Movies, like life, are full of compromise and the fight is to have as little compromise as possible. For instance, you find an ideal location in a house. You go into the study and it's kind of messed up with kids' stuff and you think 'yes, this is it!' Then they say that you can use the house but not the study. I have to tell myself it wasn't meant to be – I'll push it as far as I can but I won't say 'give them more money, I must have it!' – the point is not to interfere with the movement of all kinds of forces. Perhaps you'll go on and find something better. Compromise hurts me more than anything: you know, 'we'll have to go with it etc.' I remember the Italian location manager saying, 'The church situation is very difficult.' We'd looked at virtually every church in Venice and in most cases the script would have had to have been approved by the Vatican but we still hadn't found one. He suggested that we

construct one in a warehouse outside the city but then, on the last day of
the recce, we discovered a little church on the outskirts called Santo
Nicolo dei Mendici. I couldn't believe it. What's more it was being done
up – the scaffolding was already there – and a sign announced that it
was being paid for by the British 'Venice in Peril' fund. I couldn't believe
it. And another odd thing: three days before we were actually to shoot
the scene I went along to check the location – it was absolutely perfect,
you came out of the church and walked to that canal – and there, on a
wall, next to it was a poster advertising a Charlie Chaplin film at the
nearby cinema. When we came back the set designer had taken it down.
By that stage I'd got into this crazed groove about 'let it be', the plot is
all that is happening. It makes me feel quite nervy just thinking about it
now. I suppose I was obsessing about it. I remember thinking, am I
going barmy here? Is it right to do this or not? Anyway, we replaced the
poster. Compromise is sometimes essential but to make things easy for
yourself is to not see the real truth of that place you are in. It may be a
bit of a drag but you must force yourself to face up to the challenge. It's
the same when you are writing a script. What you think is a brilliant idea
might not turn out to be so. Yeats said, 'First, kill all your darlings.' It's
wonderful to hold onto that thought because I've found that scenes I've
loved, that were really fantastic, have ended up on the cutting-room
floor. The trick is to see what is there. There's a line in *The Treasure of
the Sierra Madre* (1948) when they have found nothing but fool's gold
and the old man is jumping up and down crying 'Theees eez eet! Theees
eez eet!' and Bogart says something like 'You don't see the gold beneath
your very feet.' It's a wonderful line. You're too busy looking, and it's
here all the time. It applies to relationships as well as film-making. For
me, once you start to impose on it the truth can die a little bit. You see
how my thoughts wander? All knowledge is connected and one thought
is connected to another but how we get there finally I don't know . . .

Was Venice an easy place to film in?

Not at all. The tides are going up and down all the time which
plays havoc with the continuity and, not only that, the equipment can't

get under the bridges at high tide. We had to keep measuring the head-room. Sometimes there were only inches and minutes to spare. I remember thinking on the recce that it was a very difficult place to shoot a film where people are supposed to be living naturally. I was determined not to show the tourist side, the side featured in endless travel documentaries, and deliberately kept out of St Mark's Square. You never see it. Venice had another part to play. Yes, it is a beautiful place but the beautiful buildings are all on the skyline and the people who live there don't go around looking at the sky. It is a maze of alleyways – that's why it's so easy to get lost – and for the most part you're in a corridor and only occasionally burst out into an open space. I didn't want to cheat. In *Lawrence of Arabia* (1962), for instance, some scenes are very beautiful but geographically impossible – i.e., what you

Roeg: 'The truth has many faces'.

see out of a window could not possibly be there. I may have been wrong but I didn't want to shoot part of a scene in one place and then shoot the reverse somewhere else. We kept getting the rushes back and all you could see was alleyways. It presented me with a terrible problem. Should I compromise or not?

Were there any other particular problems?

In some ways it was a very tough film. As *Don't Look Now* was what is called a 'deal picture', the producers were only interested in the money. I know producers have to look after the finance but in this case they had no interest at all in the film itself. Absolutely everything irritated them: they could have destroyed the picture. As the pressure increased everything got harder and harder. In the end I broke into the cutting room and took away four reels of film so they could not destroy it. Even the line producer, whose allegiance is to the producers, came up to me one evening on the verge of tears and said, 'I'm with you.' But this sort of gossip is not helpful . . . Sometimes problems crop up where you least expect them. The girl who played Christine was very pretty – exactly the sort of child John and Laura would have had – and a good swimmer too. Her mother and I took her to the swimming-pool to practise going under the water and she was perfectly happy but as soon as she saw the pond she just would not go under. She screamed and screamed. The farmer on the neighbouring farm had a daughter of a similar age and said that she was a lovely swimmer so we tried her out and she was fine but as soon as she got the red mac on she refused to go under the water. In the end we rigged it in a water tank with a double: there are actually three children in that sequence. All three, when they saw the pond and the weeds, must have felt the terrible truth: 'I'm drowning, I'm drowning.'

How did you come to cast Adelina Poerio?

That was odd, too. We had a casting session in Rome where, of course, we saw a lot of Fellini's people but then I saw Adelina's photograph. It was captivating. She was dressed as a showgirl, a perfect woman who happened to be only 4' 2". She was not a supermodel but

she was by no means unattractive. She had a career as a singer and often
stood on top of the piano during the performance. She turned up for
the audition with her lover who was of normal height – I believe she had
run away from her husband – and I remember her sitting in his lap while
he made her up and telling him to put a bit more mascara on here and
touch up her cheek there. It was marvellous to watch them. I always
think it's more horrific if someone beautiful is doing something horrible
rather than someone who is obviously ugly. It's strange . . . Adelina was
perfect and she changed with the film.

How did Don't Look Now come about originally?

The easy answer is that Allan Scott offered me the script but that's
not the whole story. It's the same with everything I've ever done: I'm
trying to make head or tail of why I like it. You read books, stories and
plays and enjoy them without knowing exactly what they're doing but
you enjoy them because they hold some truth for you. I'm very
protective about books I like. I once gave a book that I loved to an
actor. He was a very nice man but there was nothing in it that had any
connection with any truth of his and so it had no effect upon him. When
that happens I can't change my feelings about it. On the other hand,
when a friend finds similar things in a book there is no greater thrill than
having your feelings re-confirmed. That said, I don't mean that a reader
is always searching for the truth. I like working on a script, doing a film
in stages. The Witches (1989) was a children's story. I did it because of
Dahl's uncompromising, unpatronising approach and because I like
children – I do have six of my own. Castaway was a desert island story.
At first I could not get hold of it, I couldn't get a handle on how to do it
or how to make it dramatically truthful. I knew it was true for Lucy
Irvine – she'd done it – but I kept thinking, why not shoot a
documentary? Then it came to me: it was a view of a twenty-year
marriage, the falseness of people and the shell they construct. When you
first meet someone it's all, 'I like sleeping with the window open', 'Oh
yes, so do I darling', but after ten years they're saying 'Shut that bloody
window, there's a draught in here'. It was the difference between

courtship and marriage that interested me. The courtship was in London
but the marriage was in what was supposed to be paradise. With *Don't
Look Now* the hook was how a couple were affected by the loss of their
child. I like to start with a premise rather than a plot – which is not the
same thing as a message. I liked the original story very much and it
struck me that nothing is what it seems. I remember daring myself to
put it in the mouth of one of the characters. During the first week, the
only week of filming in England, I told Donald, jokingly, that he was
going to say the very premise of the movie. 'Oh God,' he said. 'Why did
you have to say that?' We had to shoot the scene fifteen times. He said
it portentously: '*Nothing* is what it *seems*.' He said it humorously. He
said it every way he could think of. In the end he said, 'I've got to put
something else in my head, I just can't think about it any more.' I told
him to forget all about it and eventually he just mumbled it. Phew! . . .
A film usually reflects things in your own life. I think it was Verlaine who
said 'I write stories and then let them happen to me.' Things don't
happen to me which I then make films about. I'm not really a proper
director that way. A director is supposed to manipulate but other people
involved have their feelings about the material too and I prefer to be
manipulated. For instance when we came to shoot the scene where
Laura lights the candles the crew said it would take a couple of hours to
set it up so I sent Julie and Donald away. After an hour Julie came back
and sat next to me and then Donald returned with a newspaper. He
strolled around and played with the light switch and said, 'I don't like
this church much' and Julie said, 'Oh, don't be silly, it's beautiful', and
I thought, that's fantastic, they've said it, that is real, it's their feeling.
But it also struck me that it was exactly what John would say to Laura
because he does not want her to be sucked back into her grief. He has
to start moving her on in life, help her to come out of her bereavement.
So we shot it like that. The original scene was quite long, two pages of
the script I think. It wasn't that we didn't need that scene – we did need
it – but it was overwritten, they had said what needed to be said and
looked at each other. Instead of joining Laura, John remains separate

from her and this is another way of helping her. It is a mutual grief but they don't go down the same avenue: one stays and one goes . . . The famous love scene – the infamous love scene – was not written either. It suddenly struck me after four weeks that John and Laura were always rowing – the candlelight dinners are over, they've had two kids and it's now more like, 'Get me a cup of tea, will you?', 'No, I'm too busy', or 'I wouldn't go in there if I were you . . .' They love each other, as the scenes in the bathroom and bedroom prove. They're not amazed by each other's nakedness, they are trying to get over a terrible thing, and in that grief nothing is what it seems. I tried the film with the scene in and with the scene out and it is a very different film without it. When the BBC first screened it they cut the scene and received letters asking for it to be put back in and, the next time they showed it, they did. It comes at a point in the movie where it is important to confirm that they are a happily married couple, that they have a good overall relationship.

Is the photograph of Ayer's Rock on the bed a coincidence?

Yes and no. I didn't deliberately search through a pile of magazines for it. It was fortuitous. Julie had this magazine and the photograph just happened to be in it. Having found it, it would have been a shame to waste the connection to *Walkabout*. It doesn't mean anything in particular, a similar example would be the Charlie Chaplin poster in *Eureka*. That said, love-making in marriage often starts by chance, you know, 'hey, look at this', you go over to see, you touch and that's it. Not everything is planned.

Have you ever attended a seance?

Yes. I wanted Julie to go to one before we started filming. Leslie Flint, the direct voice medium, used to live not far from here in Notting Hill but when I called him he said that his doctor had told him to stop working because it put such a tremendous strain on his heart. Anyway, ten days later he called to say that some American parapsychologists were coming over to observe him and that he would be happy for us to attend the session. So Julie and I went along, sat in a circle in the pitch dark and joined hands. Suddenly he said, 'Uncross your legs', and I decided to use that in the film.

Why does Wendy's silk dressing-gown slip off her knee when Heather asks Laura if her legs are crossed?

I liked the idea that there was something seductive about it, something strangely seductive, maybe even influential. Who are these women? What are they up to? . . . As a matter of fact my legs were crossed so I uncrossed them and something happened. It would have been very difficult to set up. I heard something right in my ear, between Julie and myself: 'Nicky'. No one calls me that. My family call me Nico and most of my friends call me Nic but I couldn't remember anyone ever calling me that. Afterwards Leslie said, 'I think someone was trying to reach you, Mr Roeg.' I asked if he was sure that they hadn't said Mickey but he was convinced the name had been Nicky. It was extraordinary but I couldn't think who it could have been. That evening I was having a drink with friends when one of them, a rather gentlemanly man, started to tell a boastful story. He must have been drunk or stoned but even so it was totally out of character, it just didn't make sense. The story was about an affair he had had. Julie said that she had had enough and was going to bed but told me to have another scotch if I wanted. I had one for the road then left. On the way home it came to me in a flash: I did know someone who had called me Nicky. For a few weeks a few years ago I had been very, very close to an American woman called Joan. We did not have an affair but we were very, very fond of each other. She was a vibrant, witty person. She died of cancer. I had thought about her a lot – maybe, subconsciously, I had been thinking about her that day – but I had forgotten about her. Maybe it was all in my mind. Who knows? Perhaps it really was confirming something. I was moved rather than scared.

Laura's smile at the end of the film is very moving. It's scary too. It's almost as if the second tragedy has tipped her over the edge or, coming so soon after the first, has failed to register properly. After what she – and we – have been through is there anything to smile about?

At the end of the shoot I went to see Julie and she was all dressed up for the funeral, completely swathed in black from head to toe, her face covered by a veil. I said: 'But I want to see your face, I want to see you smile.' We'd already shot the scene where Laura arrives at the hotel too late and puts her arms through the railings: 'Darlings!' I told Julie that Laura has lost her husband and her child but that she knows the two are together and happy. It is the others who are crying. Laura is in a state of grace, that's why she smiles. It is beyond their knowledge. I think it is secret and chilling, but beautiful. Emotionally, the terrible events have given her a dreadful strength. Laura is smiling at some secret memory. Relationships sometimes rot from the inside, all the bickering and petty resentment builds up a shell, a carapace that it is sometimes worthwhile trying to tear off: 'This is who I am!' Laura and John have had the best: it may be over now but it can never be taken away from them. Laura knows this. She is locked deep in some other place where superficial things like tears cannot reach her . . . As she smiles I chill. Grief takes many forms. In *Cold Heaven* things race through the mind of the widow very different to standard thought or what we think should be thought in reality. While the doctor is consoling her she moves from pragmatism – 'Who should I ring? I must tell so-and-so' – to relief – 'I'm a free woman now' – and surprise: 'Why am I not feeling anything else?' Her grief has moved her on to a new place, beyond the experience of most people. Colin Wilson tells the story of a vile, murdering beast in the Midwest, public enemy number one, who had been caught but escaped and was caught again. On the morning he was to be executed he was standing on the scaffold when the sun began to rise. Soon he felt its rays on his face. He suddenly became very calm and said: 'It *is* a beautiful world.' Then they put a hood on him and hanged him. But for thirty seconds he had seen the truth and he died with that knowledge. Some people never see it . . . When the film was finished one of the producers said, 'We're going to have to show it to Daphne du Maurier but don't be there because she doesn't know what you've done to it and we need her support.' But du Maurier was a true

writer and understood about translating a story into another medium.
I still have the letter she wrote to me. She said: 'Dear Mr Roeg, I saw
your film of my story and your John and Laura reminded me so much of
a young couple I saw in Torcello having lunch together. They looked so
handsome and beautiful and yet they seemed to have a terrible problem
and I watched them with sadness. The young man tried to cheer his wife
up but to no avail and it struck me perhaps that their child had died of
meningitis . . .' It was a wonderful letter, I know the place she meant,
too. That couple were the authors of the story. Du Maurier was not
obsessed with the big I, she didn't cry 'But it was my idea! My idea!'
The ideas are all around us; life, stories, plots are all here. The beginning
is birth, the ending is death and all the rest is just anecdote. Life does
not have a happy ending – everyone ends up dead – but movies can end
happily. Laura has survived, triumphant – death shall have no dominion
over her – their happiness may be in the past but it was real and will
always remain so. That is what you have to remember in your grief. The
truth has many faces and your truths about *Don't Look Now*, which
spring from your experience, are just as valid as mine, which spring from
my experience. In knowledge all things are connected and we each bring
different things to it. The important thing in making movies is to ensure
that the knowledge is there to be shared in the first place.

Credits

DON'T LOOK NOW

GB/Italy
1973

Production companies
D.N.L Ventures Partnership
Casey Productions
(London)/Eldorado Films
(Rome)/A Peter Katz-
Anthony B. Unger
Production

GB release
16 October 1973

Distributor
British Lion

US release
9 December 1973

Distributor
Paramount Pictures

Director
Nicolas Roeg

Executive producer
Anthony B. Unger

Producer
Peter Katz

Production Executive
Steve Previn

Associate producer
Federico Mueller

Unit manager
Franco Coduti

Production accountant
Terence O'Connor

Assistant director
Francesco Cinieri

Continuity
Rita Agostini

Casting
Miriam Brickman
Ugo Mariotti

Screenplay
Allan Scott, Chris Bryant.
Based on the short story
by Daphne du Maurier.

Photography
Anthony Richmond

Camera operator
Luciano Tonti

Assistant camera
Simon Ransley

Key grip
Spartaco Pizzi

Gaffer
Luciano Marrocchi

Editor
Graeme Clifford

Assistant editors
Tony Lawson
Peter Holt

Art director
Giovanni Soccol

Set decorator
Francesco Chianese

Wardrobe mistress
Annamaria Fea

Miss Christie's wardrobe
Marit Lieberson
Andrea Galer

Make-up
Giancarlo Del Brocco

Hair stylist
Barry Richardson

Hairdresser
Maria Luisa Garbini

Publicity
Hubert Doyle

Music
Pino Donaggio

**Music
arranger/conductor**
Giampiero Boneschi

Sound editor
Rodney Holland

Sound recording
Peter Davies

Dubbing mixer
Bob Jones

Stunt co-ordinator
Richard Grayden

Technicolor
Lenses by Panavision

110 minutes
9,883 feet

Cast:

Julie Christie
Laura Baxter

Donald Sutherland
John Baxter

Hilary Mason
Heather

Clelia Matania
Wendy

Massimo Serato
Bishop Barbarrigo

Renato Scarpa
Inspector Longhi

Giorgio Trestini
Workman

Leopoldo Trieste
Hotel manager

David Tree
Anthony Babbage

Ann Rye
Mandy Babbage

Nicholas Salter
Johnny Baxter

Sharon Williams
Christine Baxter

Bruno Cattaneo
Detective Sabbione

Adelina Poerio
Dwarf

**Available on VHS in the
UK on the Warner Home
Video label**

Bibliography

1 Source

du Maurier, Daphne, *Don't Look Now and Other Stories* (London: Penguin, 1973). A very popular collection: my copy is the nineteenth reprint. Even so it contains the unbearable typo: 'A grizzly business' (p. 39).

2 Studies

Most criticism of Nicolas Roeg is not worthy of its subject but the following either have specific things to say about *Don't Look Now* or raise interesting points about the director himself.

Feineman, Neil, *Nicolas Roeg* (Boston: Twayne, 1978). Useful discussion of the element of horror, but he believes that Nino Rota wrote the score.

Hacker, Jonathan, and Price, David, *Take Ten: Contemporary British Film Directors* (Oxford: Clarendon Press, 1991). Long essay and short interview.

Izod, John, *The Films of Nicolas Roeg: Myth and Mind* (Basingstoke: Macmillan, 1992). He bubbles with psychobabble and believes that John Barry wrote the score.

Lanza, Joseph, *Fragile Geometry: The Films, Philosophy and Misadventures of Nicolas Roeg* (New York: PAJ Publications, 1989). Brilliant and batty; by far and away the best book on Roeg but unfortunately out of print. The BFI library has a copy but if you ever come across another I will buy it off you, no questions asked.

Salwolke, Scott, *Nicolas Roeg Film by Film* (Jefferson, NC: McFarland, 1993). All right except that the dwarf is turned into a man. Do these people watch the films they write about?

Sinyard, Neil, *The Films of Nicolas Roeg* (London: Letts, 1991). Spoon-feeding for lazy students.

Walker, John, *The Once and Future Film: British Cinema in the '70s and '80s* (London: Methuen, 1983). A quick briefing in which Roeg, God help him, has to share a chapter with Ken Russell.

3 Articles, interviews and reviews

Canby, Vincent, review in *The New York Times*, 9 December 1973.

Estrin, Mark W., 'Don't Look Now' in *International Dictionary of Films and Filmmakers – 1: Films* (Chicago & London: St James Press, 1990).

Gow, Gordon, review in *Films and Filming*, November 1973.

Houston, Penelope, review in *Monthly Film Bulletin*, October 1983.

Kolker, Robert Phillip, 'The Open Texts of Nicolas Roeg', in *Sight and Sound*, Spring 1977.

Milne, Tom, review in *Sight and Sound*, Autumn 1973.

Milne, Tom, and Houston, Penelope, interview in *Sight and Sound*, Winter 1973–4.

Pirie, Dave, and Petit, Chris, 'After the Fall', in *Time Out*', 12–18 March 1976.

Variety, review, 24 October 1973.

4 Other

Feeney Callan, Michael, *Julie Christie* (London: WH Allen, 1984).Thus far the only biography of Christie ever written, which makes it all the more disappointing that the author did not get to speak with his subject. However, as cuttings-jobs go, this is a pleasant, informative picture-book. Neither Christie nor Sutherland have written an autobiography and no one has yet produced a biography of Sutherland. Don't look now . . .

BFI Modern Classics is an exciting new series
which combines careful research with high quality
writing about contemporary cinema. Authors write
on a film of their choice, making the case for its
elevation to the status of classic. The series will
grow into an influential and authoritative commentary
on all that is best in the cinema of our time.
If you would like to receive further information about
future **BFI Modern Classics** or about other books on
film, media and popular culture from BFI Publishing,
please fill in your name and address and return this
card to the BFI*.
No stamp needed if posted in the UK, Channel
Islands, or Isle of Man.

NAME

ADDRESS

POSTCODE

* North America: Please return your card to:
Indiana University Press, Attn: LPB, 601 N Morton Street,
Bloomington, IN 47401-3797   2

**BFI Publishing
21 Stephen Street
FREEPOST 7
LONDON
W1E 4AN**